A Dog's Wisdom

A Heartwarming View of Life

Margaret H. Bonham

Howell
Book House™

Howell Book House
Published by Wiley Publishing, Inc., Hoboken, New Jersey

Photo credits can be found on page 186.

For general information on our other products and services or to obtain technical support please contact our Customer Care Department within the U.S. at (800) 762-2974, outside the U.S. at (317) 572-3993 or fax (317) 572-4002.

Wiley also publishes its books in a variety of electronic formats. Some content that appears in print may not be available in electronic books. For more information about Wiley products, please visit our web site at www.wiley.com.

Library of Congress Cataloging-in-Publication Data:

Bonham, Margaret H.
    A dog's wisdom / Margaret H. Bonham.
        p. cm.
    ISBN-13: 978-0-7645-7914-1 (pbk.)
    ISBN-10: 0-7645-7914-2 (pbk.)
    1. Dogs--Miscellanea. 2. Dogs--Pictorial works. 3. Human-animal relationships. I. Title.
    SF426.2.B66 2005
    636.7'0022'2--dc22   2005003956

Printed in the United States of America

10   9   8   7   6   5   4   3   2   1

Book design by LeAndra Hosier

Cover design by Wendy Mount

Book production by Wiley Publishing, Inc. Composition Services

In memory of Quinn, Winnie, Ed, Kersel, Tasha, Houston, Lightning, Spice, Serena, Cuawn, Conan, Mirin, Shadow, Dancer, Jasmine, Skye, and Framm.
But this book is especially dedicated to Kiana, the white Malamute. If there's a heaven, she's there causing mayhem.

And to Larry, who loves the dogs as much as I do.

Contents

Acknowledgments

I'd like to acknowledge the following people for their help with the book:

Jessica Faust of Bookends.

Roxane Cerda (senior acquisitions editor), Cindy Kitchel (director of acquisitions), and Kathy Nebenhaus (publisher/vice president) of Wiley.

Beth Adelman (friend and development editor).

Myrna Wantanabe, Sandy Whelchel, Jessica Faust, Diane Peters Mayer, Carol Richtsmeier, Karen Holowinski, Charlene LaBelle for sharing stories about their dogs.

Thanks to the following people for photos: Jessica Faust, Diane Peters Mayer, Carol Richtsmeier, Al Holowinski, Karen E. Taylor, Teresa Bullard, Carolyn Risdon, Phyllis Degioia, Margaret Meleski, Monissa Whiteley, and Jim and Kathy Stabler.

Anne Page, who let me reprint recipes from *Houston's Canine Chronicles*.

Thanks to Kodiak, Kira, Haegl, and Ranger, who show me their wisdom daily. Thanks to Mishka, who has made me smile.

Thanks to Larry, who made suggestions and puts up with the dog madness.

Foreword

By Steve Dale

Dogs are wise enough to teach us simple, everyday life lessons. Just yesterday, I was putting some boxes away and I couldn't see what was going on below me because I was holding them. I accidentally stepped down pretty hard on my dog Lucy's leg. She yelped, got up, and within two seconds began to wiggle in forgiveness.

Of course, if someone mistakenly steps on our foot, we also forgive. But, now fess up: Isn't there just a tiny twinge of anger that lingers until the other person says, "Pardon me"? That's one difference between *Canis familiaris* and *Homo sapien:* Dogs forgive a whole lot faster than people do.

We've also learned to trust the judgment of our dogs. Wendy is a friend who walks through a busy Chicago park nearly every day after work. Bingo, her dog, is the type who's happy to see everyone who approaches. When he was a puppy, he tried desperately to say hi to everyone in the park, but he eventually learned not everyone wants to return the greeting or has the time to; they just keep on jogging or racing by on Rollerblades. Still, when Bingo is in the park, his tail never stops wagging.

On one winter day in the park, a man walked up to Wendy. He was about to say something, but Bingo immediately began to growl.

Wow! In Bingo's six years, Wendy had never heard that sound come from him. She looked down at her dog, totally surprised. She saw his tail was held erect and the hair on his back was standing on end.

Although all of this occurred in maybe three seconds, the stranger got the message and walked off.

The next day, a bulletin was posted in the building where Wendy lives that a man fitting exactly the description of that stranger had robbed someone in the park. It happened at around the same time Wendy and Bingo were leaving the park. Wendy believes that if it wasn't for Bingo's judgment, she would have been the one who was robbed.

Since that one cold night in the park about two years ago, Bingo has met countless people and has never growled again. How did he know?

Dogs do know things. They know how to manipulate us—even smart people who work with animals every day. My friend Annemarie Lucas, supervisory special investigator at the ASPCA and a star of *Animal Precinct* on Animal Planet, was visiting a shelter in Corpus Christi, Texas. She certainly wasn't looking for a dog; at the time she already had four. And Annemarie says if she was looking for a dog, she certainly wouldn't seek out a Dachshund and Chihuahua-type mix. "But he gave me this amazing look as if he was saying, 'You're not thinking of leaving here without me.' I don't know if I had ever seen a dog wag a tail so fast. This guy was pretty smart to get to me like that."

Today, Chet, the dog from the Texas shelter, is a part of her family.

Dogs do sometimes train us. I've interviewed several people who have seizures. Their dogs were never trained to detect the seizures, but somehow they learned to. And then they trained their owners to pay attention to them.

Just before the onset of a seizure, one dog would paw at her owner—even if was in the middle of the night. Eventually, over the course of many months, this person figured out what her dog had been saying all along. Today, she understands that when her dog paws at her in a certain way, the dog is accurately alerting her to an oncoming seizure, and she takes her medication immediately. Often, that's enough to avert the seizure.

Dogs do figure things out for themselves. Take, for example, John Vranicar's dog Kate, who is part Border Collie and part who the heck knows what else. Vranicar's partner, Colin Reeves, was driving his vehicle through Yellowood State Park in Indiana in 1997. Reeves noticed a dog in his rear-view mirror chasing after the vehicle as fast as his legs would go. He pulled over, and the approximately six-month-old pup jumped into the car as if she had just discovered a long lost friend. Colin thought he'd have a tough time convincing John to keep what would be their second dog. So instead he left the sales job up to Kate.

Vranicar recalls, "The moment I walked through the door, Kate went nuts, greeting me in a way I had never been greeted by a dog.

It's like she was saying, 'This other guy is good, but you're so much better.' Kate always knew how to work people."

Eighteen months later Kate was hit by a car, and a leg had to be amputated. But dogs don't grieve those sorts of losses the way people do, and a missing limb hasn't deterred Kate's spirit one bit.

"Kate's favorite thing is to go to the park and run up to old bag ladies or anyone who you'd think would want to have nothing to do with her," says Vranicar. "She just sits next to a person she chooses and politely wags her tail. Eventually, every bag lady winds up petting Kate and talking to her. If Kate wants to win you over, eventually she will."

Realizing Kate's empathy, Vranicar tested her to be an animal assisted therapy (AAT) dog for the Chicago-based Chenny Troupe. Kate passed the AAT test the first time around (many dogs require a few tries), and has been working with children at LaRabida Children's hospital in Chicago since 2003. Kate helps physically and developmentally disabled kids to build cognitive skills and motor function.

Vranicar says the children and even their parents especially relate to his dog because she is also handicapped. They see that she copes and does what she is able to; and she never complains if there's something to do that she can't do. "Of course, dogs have wisdom," he says.

My GPS system has four legs. Shortly after we moved into our new condominium, I noticed that no matter what direction we arrived from, our Brittany, Chaser, knows when we're near home. Even if she's totally zonked out from an all-day excursion or visit to a dog park, when we get to within about three or four blocks from the house, she pops up and looks out the window. I've tried to fool her, even intentionally passing by our home and then continuing in one direction for a mile or two before returning via another route. No matter what I try, whether we've been in the car for five hours or five minutes, Chaser knows when we're almost home. Maybe she has her own GPS system. There's so much about dogs that we're only beginning to understand.

Maggie Bonham's stories about dog wisdom are often poignant or entertaining. They are all interesting, and clearly they further my own long-standing conviction that in some ways dogs are wiser than we are.

Steve Dale is the author of the "My Pet World" syndicated newspaper column (Tribune Media Services), host of the syndicated "Steve Dale's Pet World" and "The Pet Minute," as well as "Pet Central" on WGN Radio, Chicago. Steve's website is www.petworldradio.net. Steve is a frequent pet expert on national TV, and he's a frequent speaker at veterinary conferences.

Preface

It was a cold evening in the Colorado mountains. A million stars shone above me and my sled team as we launched into the darkness along the Forest Service road. The trees loomed like ominous shadows around me and I couldn't see anything beyond my sled dogs.

I was alone, and yet there they were. Ed and Kersel in the lead. Tasha and Skye right behind them. Lightning, Jasmine, Framm, Rowdy, Junior, and Sweetie following. They were all there screaming to go, chomping lines and banging their harnesses in an effort to get me to give the command to go forward. I was alone and yet not alone. I was with the dogs.

That night I first discovered the primal link between dogs and humans. I had owned and trained dogs for many years, but had never experienced the heady rush of being part of the pack. That night was my initiation into their world. Standing on the sled, I realized what it was that made the dog.

At that moment, and in a thousand other moments since, I discovered the truth about dogs. Their wisdom and courage transcend anything we can lay claim to. They understand and know some very fundamental truths that we humans have long forgotten or have chosen to ignore. And yet, the dog's candor touches our hearts each time. Every day, dogs show us how we should live our lives. They speak to us through their hearts and loyalty and touch us in ways we never thought possible.

Some time ago—experts argue exactly when and how—dogs threw in their lot with humans. Something special within those first dogs caused us to take them into our caves or huts, feed them and keep them with our families, and eventually train them for hunting, guarding, pulling, and herding. How else could they have slipped their way into our homes and our hearts?

The modern dog is different from his ancestors, but he has the same instincts. He tells us through his actions how he looks at the world and how he thinks the world should be. This book is a collection of that canine wisdom I've seen in my own dogs, my neighbors' dogs, my friends' dogs, and, yes, even in strangers' dogs.

When you read this book, you'll step inside the world of the dog. I guarantee you'll find something to make you smile, laugh, or even become a bit teary-eyed. After all, these are dogs. Those of us who love them know they have a wisdom all their own, and they share it with us every day. Maybe you'll even see a bit of the wisdom your own dog has whispered to you.

Meet the Dogs with Wisdom

Throughout this book, you'll be receiving tips from four very clever dogs: Kodiak, Kira, Haegl, and Ranger. Each one of them imparts a bit of their wisdom and, hopefully, a bit of their personality and sense of humor.

Kodiak

Kodiak

Kodiak is a purebred Alaskan Malamute who is seven years old. He likes to think he's in charge of everything in the house, but when it comes right down to it, he's a big mush pie. Just don't tell him that! Kodiak likes hiking, backpacking, food balls, walks, and being bossy.

Kira

Kira and Larry

Kira is sitting here with Larry, my husband. She's a seven-year-old Alaskan Malamute and is Kodiak's sister. Don't be fooled by her sweet expression. She's really the one who is in charge. Kira likes food, bossing all the other dogs around, the couch, figuring out tricks so she can get more food, and occasional walks. But she'd rather be home on the couch.

Ranger

anger is a German Shepherd Dog who we found in the middle of the road. (His story is in this book.) He's about nine years old and is still very unsure of himself.

Ranger

Haegl

This is Haegl and me. He's a two-year-old bundle of energy who loves everyone and everything, until they show any attitude with him. He's the only dog in my house with his own journal (see it at www.havingfunwithagility.com), and he loves hiking, backpacking, agility, climbing ladders, playing practical jokes, and visiting with people.

Haegl and Maggie

1
A Dog's Life

What is it exactly that makes us humans envious of a dog's life? Is it because deep down inside we know that our dogs lead happy, simple lives? That they don't need to seek a wise man on top of a mountain to find themselves, because they know exactly where they are? That they have no worries to speak of—no bills, business meetings, final exams, or power lunches? That they're not interested in impressing a new girlfriend or boyfriend and they're not angry if you missed their birthday?

We could learn a few things from our dogs. I know I could. One of my dogs is always telling me to take a break and enjoy life. After all, what could be easier than living in the moment?

Live Spontaneously

Boomer, a yellow Labrador Retriever, greeted us with a big smile. He carried a stick that was much too large—nearly as long as his body. First, he gave me the stick to throw. I threw it and he leaped after it. He caught it neatly in the air, then brought it back and gave it to my husband, Larry, to throw. Larry threw it as far as he could, and Boomer scampered after it and brought it back to me. And so it went.

Boomer didn't know us, but he clearly decided it was more fun to make up his own game on the spot than to just hang out. Perhaps he was waiting for his owner to arrive as he brought each stick back—first to me, then to Larry. Anyway, we all had fun.

> **Kodiak says . . .**
> It's never a good idea to let dogs run loose. A dog can bother the neighbors or be hit by a car.

Surprise Someone with Something You've Learned

Haegl the Malamute peered into the bathroom window. His mask and dark eyes made him look like a bandit as he peeked in. He wagged his head from side to side in a doggy grin.

I was washing my hands in the bathroom when I saw him—the *upstairs* bathroom! I rushed outside to see him balancing on a ladder that lay against the side of the house. It had snowed recently and the snow had anchored the ladder in place. Earlier that day, we climbed the ladder to knock the snow off the roof and Haegl watched. Maybe a little too well.

> *Haegl says . . .*
>
> **Don't leave things out that dogs can get into. We'll surprise you with our ingenuity.**

He had put one foot on each rung and had climbed up far enough to peer into the bathroom window.

"Come down from there!" I said. And Haegl hopped down, laughing as he did. It was a great joke!

Be Who You Are

*C*onan was a black Newfoundland-Samoyed mix with long hair and one ear that would stick straight up and another that would flop over. He hated obeying commands but loved to pull, just like his sled dog ancestors.

One day I put a sled dog harness on him. He hung back, eyeing me curiously, thinking I would correct him for pulling. Instead, I

encouraged him. He began a little prance with his front feet, tossing his head like a horse who has finally been given enough rein. He laid his ears flat and pulled. And pulled. And pulled. When we stopped, he turned to me with a big smile.

He was good at this! I let him be who he wanted to be, instead of trying to make him something he wasn't. He needed to follow his own way, not mine.

Howl at the Moon

A lone howl rose, carried on the wind. The moon was only partly lit and peeked through the autumn clouds. Another howl, then another rose.

The song came first from the coyotes along the bluffs of the valley, their silver muzzles and yellow eyes gleaming in the bright moonlight. One by one, the dogs answered the call. Cody's shrill tenor mixed with Razor's deep baritone as the Huskies began their wild serenade. The dogs across the valley picked up the call: a Collie, two St. Bernards, another Husky, and a mixed breed all lifted their heads. They sang with pure passion for the song.

When it was over, they wagged their tails and pranced in play. No reason, really, for all that howling. Doing something for the passion of it is sometimes all that matters.

Take a Siesta

It's midday and my Alaskan Malamutes are quiet. They're all taking a siesta.

Kira lies with her legs in the air and her lips drawn back in a smile. Kodiak lies on the cool tiles, his eyes half shut and his toes stretched ever so slightly. Haegl snores beneath my desk, his ears occasionally twitching. Lazy dogs? Hardly. They know how to beat the summer's heat.

Dogs sleep twelve to sixteen hours a day. Naps are a way to recharge. As soon as it gets a bit later, and cooler, they'll be active and ready to go. Sometimes a nap is all you need to regain your energy.

Stick to a Schedule

Dogs are creatures of habit. It's comforting to know when things will happen and it gives them something to look forward to. Look at your dog. He knows when it's dinnertime. He knows when you go to work, when you come home, and when you walk him. Whether it's playtime or dinnertime, dogs know.

> *Haegl says . . .*
>
> **Walk your dog every day. It's healthy for both of you.**

Haegl wakes me up around eight o'clock every morning. Kira knows breakfast is at 8:30. If Larry's home, it's long walk day. Afternoon is siesta time. Dinner is at 5:30. Last time out is at 10 P.M.

Establish a schedule. Things are less complicated.

There's Safety in Numbers

reeowowerrrr!" Cuawn barked. The blue merle Australian Shepherd stood by the fence with his hackles up. Beside him stood Conan, the Newfoundland-Samoyed mix; Shadow, the Keeshond; and Mirin, the Siberian Husky mix.

The scary man approached the fence. Cuawn looked from side to side. Conan had puffed himself up—a veritable wall of black fur. Shadow yapped loudly—how dare this man try to enter the backyard! Mirin glared at him with her icy blue eyes. Alone, Cuawn would never stand his ground, but with four buddies, he was not afraid.

The man backed down and went around to the door. I heard the doorbell and peered out the window.

"Can you get the meter readings?" he asked sheepishly.

As I walked around to the back, my four protectors followed me. Cuawn strutted beside me, proud of having made that man back down.

Hang Tough

Sandy Whelchel told me about her dog, Ebony, a black Labrador Retriever, and the strength some dogs have. Ebony was six months old when she got out of her yard and ran in front of a car in their rural neighborhood in Colorado.

"It wasn't just a small car," Sandy said, "but a full-size Nissan." Sandy saw the whole accident happen, and the car ended up on top of Ebony. "I could see from the house that she was still alive, but I was heartbroken because there seemed no way she could survive that and I felt sure I'd have to put her down."

Sandy's husband, Andy, ran out with a jack and cranked the car off the dog. Ebony leaped up and raced around the outside of the house three times before waiting for Sandy to let her in at the back door. Sandy quickly rushed Ebony to the veterinarian.

With the exception of a couple of gashes—one that was eight inches long—the vet pronounced Ebony fit. Sandy cared for Ebony. Each day, Sandy washed her wounds with antibacterial soap and Ebony stood stoically without whimpering or snapping. By the end of a week, the wounds had healed perfectly.

"That dog taught me a lot," Sandy said. "Ebony taught me how to hang tough."

Whining Works

"Squeak, squeak!" said Shadow. He stared out of his crate. It was morning now—why wasn't his owner coming upstairs to let the dogs out?

The other dogs waited patiently in their crates as Shadow squeaked. Conan exchanged glances with Cuawn. They knew the game.

"Shhh!" came their owner's voice.

"Squeak, squeak!" whined Shadow.

"Shhh!"

"Squeak!"

"All right," said his owner as she appeared to let them out. "Yes, I'll take you for a walk."

Love Is Stronger than Death

I don't believe in ghosts. I've never gone to a psychic. I scoff at *Sightings*. I tell you this up front because I don't have a good explanation for what happened. But maybe, just maybe, the bond between a person and a dog can be so intense that it can reach beyond death.

"Kiana has bone cancer," Jim announced. Jim had been my vet for a long time, and I trusted his diagnosis. "It's not arthritis like we thought. The problem is where the cancer is—it's not very treatable and the prognosis isn't good."

I stared in shock at Kiana, who lay there in pain. Kiana was a white Alaskan Malamute and had been my best friend for thirteen years. She had a handful of agility and working titles and did everything I asked of her.

The symptoms had started innocuously enough—a small limp. But she was thirteen—old for a Malamute. We had treated her with anti-inflammatories and, for a while, the limp had gotten better. But now she was in terrible pain.

"We'll treat the pain," I said, feeling awful. "When the pain medicine no longer works, I'll put her to sleep."

The pain became too intense after four days, and Kiana and I saw Jim again.

After the euthanasia, I tossed Kiana's collar in my SUV. I didn't want to think about her death and I didn't want to think about her. Instead, I threw myself into the book I was writing. But little things kept reminding me of her. At night, I'd dream of her (something that never happened with other dogs I'd had to euthanize), and when I looked at her empty crate, for a brief second I'd see a white Malamute standing there. I thought I was losing my mind.

Then, one evening when I got home and was opening the front door of my house, my parked SUV started moving toward me. I leaped out of the way, then opened the car door to find the gear lever had been knocked into drive. I put the gear into park and put the parking brake on.

Funny, I thought. *Kiana used to knock cars into gear all the time.*

The next day I received a phone call from the vet telling me that Kiana's ashes were ready to be picked up. I drove down to the vet's office, occasionally glimpsing something white in the back of my SUV in my rearview mirror. I took the ashes and drove home.

When I got home, I took Kiana's ashes out and then decided to fold the seats up so people could sit in the car again. As I folded the car seats up, I stared at the gift Kiana had left in the car for me: a big gourmet biscuit I had given her about a month before. I usually don't buy these, so I recognized it immediately. I had watched her eat it the day I got it for her. And yet, here it was.

I picked up the biscuit and then searched for her collar, finding it on the passenger seat. I took the collar, ashes, and biscuit and lay them on my desk, where I spend a large portion of my time (and where she used to lie under at my feet). The odd occurrences and glimpses of white fur stopped. I had one more dream about her, in which she was happy to be beside me once more.

I suppose I could explain all the strange things away: I left the car in gear, Kiana didn't really eat that biscuit, and I was imagining she was here when she wasn't. Even if those incidents can be explained, I'm not going to try. There are some bonds between humans and dogs that need no explanation. And there is a love that reaches beyond even death.

Try Something Scary

*S*plash!
Sadie the Pit Bull mix stared at the wading pool, quivering. She was terrified of the water, but there was something about the pool she found irresistible. She edged closer, watching the light dance on the patterns beneath the water. The sunlight glinted, making the surface shimmer and dance.

She poked her nose at the water cautiously. There they were again: pretty shapes beneath the water. They rippled and moved each time she touched the water. She stuck a paw in tentatively. And again. What were those things on the bottom?

She stepped in and began to paw them, no longer afraid of the pool.

> **Ranger says...**
>
> Baby pools are great, but big pools can be dangerous. Keep unsupervised dogs away from big pools and teach your dog how to walk out of the pool on his own when you're both enjoying it.

Be Curious

*W*aves rumbled over the sands as Serena the Collie walked along the beach. The sun was setting, and while the sand was still warm, it had cooled enough for her tender paws. She spent some time chasing the waves as they rolled in and out again.

The briny smell of the ocean filled her nostrils, along with another smell she wasn't familiar with. Something odd. She walked over to a pile of sand to see it scuttle away. She blinked, not believing her eyes.

Serena caught another movement in the corner of her eye. What was that? A lump of sand scuttled away from her again. It was a ghost crab—a crab the color of the sand, which only comes out in the evenings and at night. The crab scurried into its hole.

Serena now saw the game. She chased all the crabs back into their holes. What a great game! And she wouldn't have discovered it if she hadn't been curious.

Taste Everything

*F*erdi, the Shetland Sheepdog puppy, was curious. He was in his new backyard and there were all sorts of unfamiliar and exciting things to smell and taste. He tried a little of the grass clippings, then the leaves and some pine needles. Munch, munch. Everything was new.

These things aren't necessarily good for a puppy, but Ferdi learns about them by tasting them. He's open-minded about things and will decide by experience if he likes them or not.

Thankfully, we have more sense than a puppy, knowing what is safe and what is not, but we've lost a bit of our adventurous spirit when it comes to eating things. Maybe you've never tasted caviar or sushi or tofu. Like Ferdi, you'll never know if they're tasty until you try them.

> ### Kira says . . .
> Dogs don't know what's poisonous. Keep all dangerous items out of reach and don't use lawn and garden chemicals that can be licked off or absorbed through the skin. Certain foods and beverages are dangerous to dogs, too. These include chocolate, onions, raisins, grapes, alcohol, raw salmon, and anything with caffeine.

Be Amazed

Conan stood perfectly still, looking up into the sky. He had never seen such a strange sight. The gray sky was filled with white flakes, falling down thick and fast. They covered his black fur, turning it white. The swirling flakes fell into his eyes, making him blink, and melted on his tongue. What was this marvelous stuff?

I laughed as I saw him, and scooped up a handful of the fluffy white powder and tossed it at him. The snow exploded in his face and he hopped back for a second. He nosed the snow and found that it moved. It tasted good, too.

I tossed a snowball into a drift and he ran after it, throwing himself in. He found himself swimming through a sea of white. Turning around, he bounded back and I threw another snowball for him to chase. Around and around he went, laughing as he did.

He had discovered snow!

2
That Denning Instinct

Dogs know the value of home. It's a comfortable place to share with loved ones. A soft cushion to curl up on during cold winter days, watching your favorite movie on television with a crackling fire in the fireplace. A place of refuge when thunder rumbles in the sky and the cold rain pelts the window with sharp splats. A place to enjoy family and friends when they gather. And of course, a place to enjoy dinner.

Dogs love the security of home. They feel safe when they're with their loved ones—safe enough to joyously greet new friends and warn off intruders. They know that denning is the right thing to do when they're sick and coming home is just as important as exploring the world.

Never Dirty Your Den

*T*asha cleaned her newborn puppies thoroughly. The Alaskan Husky was nursing three red puppies and one gray one. The whelping box was small, but warm and cozy like a den. Tasha knew keeping her puppies clean helped ensure their survival. She pushed the soiled newspapers and blankets aside, away from the puppies, until her humans had a chance to clean them up.

When she had to relieve herself, she left the whelping box to go outside. When she came back, she continued her fastidious caretaking by gently washing each of the puppies and cleaning up after them.

Have you ever wondered why dogs are housetrained so much faster when you confine them in a crate or a small space? Like wolves, dogs have a natural instinct that tells them never to soil their den if they can help it. How long has your Mom been trying to teach you that one?

> *Haegl says . . .*
>
> **You can teach your dog to ring a bell when he needs to go outside. Just hang a bell by the door and every time you let him out, point to the bell until he noses it. Before long, he'll be ringing the bell to let you know he needs to go out.**

Home Is Where You Enjoy Family and Friends

It was snowing outside and Ranger the German Shepherd lay by the crackling wood stove. The other dogs—all Alaskan Malamutes—had gone outside for a romp in the snow, but Ranger decided instead to stay warm by the fire. Hailey the cat joined him, lying next to him to keep warm.

He closed his eyes as he felt Hailey's rough tongue against his fur. She quietly groomed him as he lay beside her, enjoying her company and her friendship.

Home Is a Safe Place

*B*oom! The house shook as thunder rolled off the hills. Ranger quivered in fear. Another flash—followed by a louder boom—resonated through the house. He shook again, almost catatonic with fear.

He had always been like this. In a previous home he had been left outside on a chain to endure the violent thunderstorms that roll across the Rocky Mountains in the summertime. He knew when they were coming. There was always a hint of ozone in the air, a dimness in the light, and a distant thunder rumble that heralded the coming of one of the big storms.

Ranger says . . .

Did someone say "thunder"? That's a very scary thing! Dogs who are afraid of thunder need help from a behaviorist and are best put in their crates when a storm brews, so they're in a safe place.

The other dogs watched him with mild curiosity. They weren't afraid the way he was. Haegl tried to play with him, to get Ranger's mind off the successive booms that echoed through the valley. "Let's go outside and bark at it," he said to the frightened German Shepherd. "You'll see, it'll be great fun."

Ranger slunk away and returned to his crate—a safe haven—and crouched inside. Right now, he couldn't be in a better place than his den.

Know the Way Home

"Where are we?" I asked Serena. We had just moved from Virginia to Colorado and everything was new. We had gone on what I thought was a short walk, but we'd taken a few too many turns and had gotten turned around. I really didn't know where we were. "Can you go home?" I asked her. "Do you know the way home?"

The beautiful sable and white Collie looked up at me in amazement. *How could a human be so silly?* she wondered. She started trotting down the road the way we came. She paused and sniffed the air occasionally or stopped briefly to look behind her to make sure I was keeping up.

We walked down many streets until at last I recognized the surroundings. When we were a block away from our new home, I stopped and hugged her. She knew the way!

Protect Your Home

The couple woke to hear the puppies barking—again. It wasn't normal for the two six-month-old mixed breeds to bark like this. And this time it sounded more urgent. Someone was trying to break in.

The barking turned to snarling, and they could hear something scrape along the front door. The woman huddled in bed, afraid. The puppies were no match against an intruder. If he got in, he would see that they were just puppies.

She turned on the outside security light. Suddenly there were footsteps—running away. A car door slammed and a vehicle sped off.

The woman and man ran to the puppies and held them close. Young but very vocal, they knew what to do. They could already protect their family's home.

Celebrate the Holidays

innamon always knew when the holidays came around. Maybe it was the crisp fall air or the scent of cinnamon—his namesake—inside the house. Maybe it was the bright wrapping paper or the laughter and high spirits of his family.

The big Golden Retriever would get a little extra turkey around Thanksgiving—that was the first sign. As the air grew colder, Cinnamon knew his people would get silly. They'd dress him up in costumes along with his two canine friends, Ginger and Audrey. And then there was the Christmas tree with loads of brightly colored packages underneath. As he sniffed, he could smell the treats inside: doggie cookies for each of them. He snuffled at a large green package. This one contained rawhide bones. What was in that package? A stuffed toy?

One morning, his humans got him up early and Cinnamon quickly realized it was time for presents—but not yet! His humans dressed him up in an odd costume. What was it?

Audrey and Ginger grinned at him with big Golden smiles. Cinnamon was now Santa Paws! He oversaw his humans as they handed out each of the presents for the dogs to unwrap. He watched with glee as Audrey unwrapped her present and devoured her cookies. Ginger was chewing her bone.

> *Kira says . . .*
> Don't forget your dog around the holidays. There are extra temptations such as Christmas trees, lights and cords, mistletoe, and turkey bones, all of which can be deadly to dogs. Give your dog a present and keep him safe over the holidays!

"Wait, Cinnamon!" his owners said. "Here's your present!"

Cinnamon stared at the bright gold package before tearing into it. Something warm and fuzzy greeted his mouth. He pulled it out. His own teddy bear!

Cinnamon got other treats as well. As he settled down beside the tree for a nap that evening, he snuggled with his new favorite toy. A squeaky teddy bear.

Home Is a Great Place to Cuddle

It's cold outside and the snow is falling. The wood stove is warm with a crackling fire and I have a hot cup of cocoa and a favorite video on the television. As I sit on the couch, Kodiak slips beside me and slides his massive head into my arms. Soon, my 110-pound Alaskan Malamute is in my lap, getting hugs.

We watch the movie together, warmed by each other's company, as the wind howls outside and the snow swirls in dizzying patterns.

Defend Your Turf

"*B*ar-rar-rar-ra!*" Maynard, the coyote told us. He was as big as a midsize dog, with agouti fur and a lanky build. He made his home among the pine and aspen trees, just outside of a little field. He lifted his lips in a snarl as he eyed the humans and dogs who had invaded his territory. He barked and yipped. Maynard would sometimes make a sudden charge and stop a few feet away, barking wildly. "This is my turf!" he said.

Kodiak and Kira, my two Malamutes, were nonplussed. They wagged their tails. "Don't worry," they seemed to say. "We're just passing through."

Maynard escorted us to the end of his territory, lagging ten feet behind. He let us know when we were outside it with a single snort and a leg lift. "My territory!" Maynard said with one more loud bark before we left for good.

Maynard returned to his den and heard the contented whimpers of three little coyote pups, their eyes not yet open. Momma Coyote licked his jaw as Maynard nuzzled her affectionately. He touched noses with each of the pups, letting each one become familiar with his scent, before turning to go out again on patrol.

3

Marking Territory

Dogs have a unique perspective on what's theirs and what's yours. Dogs guard their home jealously, but they allow friends and family to enter it with joy. Their property seems to extend to things they see and places they go. It's not unusual for a dog to claim familiar places as an extension of his territory.

Dogs are also natural thieves. If you've ever had your dinner swiped off the table or a counter raided, you know how unabashed they are when it comes to stealing. A stolen meal now is worth any price paid later.

Perhaps some of the lessons they teach us in this chapter aren't the best. Kira and Kodiak don't feel a whit of guilt when they steal bacon, but they do dread getting caught. Being very possessive of things isn't good either, but dogs tend to be anyway. It's in their nature. It's in our nature, too, but dogs are more honest about it.

Think Big

Bud, a little Schipperke mix, eyed the basket of fruit as it sat on the kitchen counter. The scents coming from the basket were exquisite. He could smell the apples, bananas, and oranges—all which he loved.

He could almost taste the banana, skin and all. The juicy orange and the crisp, tart apple made his mouth water. If he stood on his tippy toes, he could just barely reach the counter. He snuck closer and stretched his neck toward the fruit. Could he reach it? Bud stretched as far as he could and his teeth snagged the stem of an apple. He pulled slowly and it rocked the basket. He tried again, but the apple got hung up on the edge of the basket.

Could he get the apple? Bud pulled and the basket tipped. The apple came spinning out and bounced off the counter and onto the floor. Bud took one bite and, lodging the apple between his teeth, dragged his prize away. It was nearly as big as he was!

What's Mine Is Mine

Bruce the Golden Retriever was chewing on his rubber bone when Tyler, his Dachshund buddy, came into the room. Bruce gripped the rubber toy in his paws a little tighter and chewed on it a little harder.

Tyler eyed the bone curiously. "What ya got there?" Tyler asked with his body language.

Bruce chewed harder on the bone. "Mine! Mine!" he said.

Tyler looked at the tennis balls in the toy box. He picked one out of the box, walked over to Bruce, and dropped the ball next to Bruce so that it bounced a couple of times and then rolled until it hit Bruce's paw. "Play?" Tyler asked, wagging his tail.

Bruce ignored the tennis ball. "Mine," he said, chewing his bone.

Tyler went back to the toy box and pulled out his own bone. He wasn't going to trick Bruce today.

What's Yours Should Be Mine

Kira and Haegl lay together on the family room floor, chewing their big marrow bones. Haegl eyed Kira's bone—was it better than his? It looked bigger. Maybe it was.

He chewed his own bone half-heartedly. How come she got the better bone? He looked at his bone. Maybe he could switch them

when she wasn't looking. Maybe he could offer it to her in exchange. Could she tell the difference in size?

He snuck over to Kira, slowly pushing his bone toward hers. Maybe he could grab hers when she wasn't looking. Kira continued to chew her bone, seemingly oblivious to Haegl's attempt to abscond with her prize. He crept nearer and nearer . . .

With a snarl, Kira grasped Haegl's bone and pulled it to her. She pushed her own bone under her legs so he couldn't get it either, and started chewing his bone. Haegl stood up in shock. She had taken *his* bone.

My Land—I Protect It

Geordi, an Australian Shepherd–Labrador Retriever mix, came running down the side of the hill. He was a midsize dog with a wavy golden coat and a bobbed tail. His hackles were up and he barked loudly as I walked by.

"This is my property! Stay away!" he barked. He kept to the perimeter of his property and followed me as I walked by.

Satisfied that I wasn't intent on doing mischief, Geordi snuffed loudly and walked back up the hill, occasionally glancing behind to make sure I wasn't going to return. Ready at a moment's notice, I knew Geordi would return every time I did to remind me this was *his* home.

If It's on the Ground, It's Mine

Clio the Border Collie sniffed the ground. Something smelled wonderful nearby. Her friend, Benny, a Bassett Hound–Beagle cross, was playing with her when her nose caught the scent. What was it?

Clio followed her nose into the bushes, with Benny following. Along with the heady smell of earth and summer flowers came the unmistakable smell of something tasty. *What is it?* she wondered.

She poked her head into the bushes. A little farther, her nose told her. She slipped deeper into the bushes. And then her teeth touched it.

Clio popped out of the bushes carrying a rawhide bone.

"Look what I found!" she said. "It's mine! I found it! It's mine!"

Eat All Your Food

"Are you going to finish that?" Quinn the Malamute asked.

It was a warm July day in the mountains and Larry sat down for lunch after a long hike up the trail. Quinn was with him. Larry pulled Quinn's backpack off and poured water for the dog into his collapsible trail bowl, then took a swig for himself. Then Larry gave Quinn some biscuits before pulling out his own peanut butter sandwich.

> **Kira says . . .**
>
> Dogs love treats! Just make sure they add up to no more than 5 percent of their total daily calories.

He was sitting and enjoying the view of the mountains as he was eating, never noticing the stealthy Malamute creeping up on him.

Larry took a bite and then another. And then suddenly his sandwich was gone!

Quinn smacked his lips as he finished the last bit of crust. "You have any more?" he asked.

Know Your Territory

erena the Collie would see someone walking along the sidewalk and bark. Although she was loose in her yard, she knew where the yard ended and the sidewalk began. She also knew where the neighbors' yards began.

> **Kodiak says . . .**
>
> Don't let your dog run loose, no matter how smart he is. Dogs need the security of a fenced-in yard.

Knowing the boundaries of your territory isn't that difficult, even when there are no obvious boundary markers. Dogs are observant—they can see subtle changes in the land such as different types of grass. Serena recognized those changes and knew her territory very well.

"This is my territory!" she barked to the world. She walked along the border of the yard like a surveyor and never set a paw over the line.

Guard Your Possessions

*D*ixie, the white Bull Terrier, grumbled loudly at her brother Moose. Dixie was carrying her favorite tennis ball in her mouth and Moose wanted it.

Moose pawed at Dixie's mouth, wagging his tail so hard that it smacked against the wall with a loud thump, thump, thump. Dixie turned away sharply. "My toy!" she said with a louder growl. "Go find your own."

Moose glanced at the toy bin. The toys there weren't as cool as the one Dixie was carrying. He pestered her for a bit, until Dixie took her tennis ball and left the room. Moose lay down and sighed. He'd have no fun stealing stuff today.

> **Haegl says . . .**
>
> Stealing toys is a lot of fun, but it can often cause fights. Don't let one dog bully another.

Turn Your Back and It's Mine

Kira and Kodiak watched as the bacon sizzled on the stove. The aroma was intense and they sniffed the air in anticipation. I scooped the bacon out of the frying pan and set it on a paper lined plate.

As I turned my back to find a jar to put the fat in, Kira edged toward the counter. She knew she had only a moment. She seized the paper towel in her teeth and pulled the bacon to the floor. I turned around to find two Alaskan Malamute juvenile delinquents munching merrily on the bacon and the paper towel.

"Mmmm" is all Kira said when I confronted her.

> *Kira says . . .*
>
> **Even the best-behaved dog can be tempted, so keep all temptations out of nose reach. Many dog owners stash food in the microwave, oven, or refrigerator to keep it safe.**

4

Working Dogs

Dogs, like people, need a job to do. Whether it's guarding a home, herding sheep, leaping over agility hurdles, pulling a sled, or searching for someone who is lost, dogs were bred to work. They do not enjoy being unemployed.

Humans probably first used dogs for hunting, herding, and pulling sleds or carts. Later, we discovered the versatility of dogs and they became more specialized in their work. Some became guard dogs; others were good at rooting out vermin. The hunting dogs specialized: some flushed out game; others were sent to chase the game alone or in packs; still others were used to point and retrieve. Other dogs did their best work as companions—but that certainly doesn't mean they had no job at all.

It has only been within the last century that the dog's role has changed from worker to pet. Not all dogs have made the change willingly; every year, hundreds of thousands of dogs are relinquished to shelters because they show working aptitude but not pet aptitude. Dogs, like people, need a job to do or they become bored. And bored dogs can be annoying and destructive. Give them a job to do, though, and you'll be amazed at how fast and how willingly they learn.

We can learn so much from our canine companions when it comes to working with others. The dog is the quintessential pack animal; he feels more secure when he is working toward a shared goal. Watch how your dog goes about his work—no matter what that work is. You can learn a lot from him.

Leaders Don't Always Look the Part

Ed was the ugliest Husky you'd ever seen. He looked like somebody's junkyard mutt, with a black and tan coat, rat tail, and ears that lay on the side of his head. People would pass him by as an ugly mutt and pet my prettier dogs with blue eyes and classic Husky masks.

But Ed had a secret. He had a heart of pure gold and was a dynamite lead sled dog. In fact, he was the closest thing I had ever come to a perfect leader. He would die before giving up.

I was running a middistance race in Idaho that was twenty-five miles each day. Ed was my lead dog. On the second day, he began to have a hitch in his gait. He wasn't limping, but he wasn't running the way I was used to. I put him in the sled so he could ride. But Ed had other ideas. He barked and barked at me as he tried to get out and take his place in the front of the team, which was struggling on without him. I looked into those brown, soulful eyes and knew he had to lead. He wouldn't give up; this race was important to him.

I took him off the sled and rubbed him down. He went right to the front of the team and waited for me to hook him up. "Let's finish this!" he seemed to say. "Let's do it!"

We finished the race. Last but not least. I hugged him and he licked my face. "Thank you," Ed's eyes said.

The veterinarians looked him over and declared that he had arthritis in his hips—nothing major, but it would keep him from racing. I knew it was time for him to retire now. I was not so sure Ed agreed.

Be Patient

Where's that squirrel?

Sadie the Pit Bull mix saw the squirrel scamper across the yard. At first she tried to chase it, but the little gray creature scrambled up the tree trunk just out of reach, flicking his tail and chattering in indignation. She stared at the tree trunk, willing it to become shorter, but it did not bend to her will.

She sat down and waited. The squirrel scrambled up into the branches, chittering as it went. Sadie waited, slowly scratching an itch on her shoulder and yawning. She would wait. She had all day.

Act Like You Know What You're Doing

Slider the coyote was crossing the local airport runway. He watched the runway, keeping an eye out for incoming airplanes rather than looking straight ahead. He trotted quickly—and ran smack into a light pole and bounced off. He shook himself and glared at the pole for a moment before continuing on as though nothing happened.

If a coyote can feel embarrassment, I suspect Slider did. But he kept his cool and went on his way. And he held his head high as if to say, "I meant to do that!"

Leadership Takes Many Forms

When people see me with my sled dogs, they often ask who my lead dog is. I tell them I have at least five lead dogs. This puzzles them, but it shouldn't. Like people, dogs are gifted in certain areas. And just as you seldom meet someone who is both a good plumber and a good carpenter, you seldom have a dog who is good at leading in every condition all the time. There are trail leaders who know how to run down a trail and do it fast. There are lead dogs who know how to pace a team for a long race. There are lead dogs who know how to turn right and left. There are also lead dogs who you can always rely on when the going gets tough.

Houston is my left-hand leader. He's an older black and tan sled dog with flop ears and a Beagle face. He knows "haw" (left turn) and that's good enough for him. He knows how to stop and go on command, too. But he doesn't care much about right turns. Cheyenne, my bossy little leader, knows "gee" (right turn). She's pure white and looks like a little Greyhound. She knows how to move forward quickly but likes to have the security of another dog beside her. She's very dependable.

Rigel knows "gee" and knows how to follow a trail. He has blue eyes and a Husky face with a demonic look about him. He knows if

I don't catch him in the act, he can get away with goofing off. Calvin is my go-fast dog and knows "haw." He's Rigel's buddy and together they're cut-ups.

Razor is my "I'll lead when others won't" dog. I've relied on him a few times. He's the analyst of the group, constantly coming up with new ideas.

Some of my dogs don't mind leading through bad weather; others will wilt. Still others only like working with certain other dogs. A dynamite leader who runs fast down a relatively straight trail may not be a good dog for a trail with lots of turns. There are those who can lead in some circumstances but not in others. Leadership is like that.

Lead When You Know the Way

Kiana the white Alaskan Malamute waited impatiently. She had her red backpack on and was ready to go. She walked in circles around me impatiently as she waited for the others in our hiking group to get ready.

"Hurry up!" she said. "We're burning daylight!" She pulled on her leash and looked expectantly at me.

We started out slowly and Kiana dragged me forward, past the other Malamutes. We walked down the rocky trail, surrounded by blue spruce, pines, conifers, and aspen. She caught the sweet scent of summer in the air—the heady aroma of warm pine needles and wildflowers. A bee buzzed by and she paused for a moment to look behind. The other Malamutes and their owners were coming now.

"I know the way!" Kiana said, waving her plume tail like a flag. She looked behind at me and wagged her head. "We're going to have fun!"

Haegl says . . .

Backpacking with dogs is loads of fun, and you can do day hikes, too. Check out Charlene LaBelle's book *A Guide to Backpacking with Your Dog*.

Be Tenacious

*M*ine! Mine!" Sadie said.

Sadie saw her owner holding the tug ball and grabbed on. She pulled and pulled. Her owner backed up, pulling hard as well.

Sadie held on and closed her eyes. "My toy!" she said and braced herself. She pulled hard and spun around, finally pulling the toy from her owner.

With a satisfied "wuff," Sadie lay down with the toy across her neatly crossed front legs.

Be Nice to Those Below You

Cuawn the Australian Shepherd watched as Mirin and Shadow played together. Mirin was a little white mutt with short hair and bright blue eyes. Shadow was a Keeshond with long gray fur and spectacles. Mirin leaped around, growling in play, before making a bow and wagging her tail furiously. Shadow made a play bow as well and leaped away, letting little Mirin chase him across the yard.

Then Cuawn joined in. Mirin stood there fearfully for a moment as the big blue merle Australian Shepherd walked up to them. Shadow quavered a bit, but Cuawn bent in a play bow. Mirin's ears pricked up. She bowed to him and Cuawn turned and ran, barking with great delight as he did. He pivoted and turned to chase her. Mirin skittered to a halt and then ran off, being followed by the Australian Shepherd.

Soon, they were all playing merrily, despite their differences in pack order. When they stopped to rest, they all laid down in the warm summer afternoon with tongues lolling.

Expect Good Things from People

Sadie knew what time it was. She got up, stretched, and pawed at the door. Then she looked up at her owner with wide brown eyes and placed a paw gently on her knee.

"It's almost time," she pleaded.

Sadie's owner let her out. Sadie ran to the mailbox and lay down. *Will he come? Will he come?*

Sadie knew he would. She waited expectantly as the minutes slipped past. Five minutes. Ten minutes. Soon nearly half an hour had passed.

Then she heard the faint rumble of the mail truck and the crunch of tires on gravel. The mail carrier drove up to her mailbox and Sadie was on her feet. He sorted through the mail and opened the box, sliding the mail in. Then he looked at Sadie.

"Have you been a good girl?"

Sadie wagged her tail. The mail carrier pulled out a biscuit and handed it to her.

She took the treat and wriggled all over as he waved good-bye. She headed back inside, knowing she could expect another treat tomorrow.

Think before You Act

osha the Pomeranian lay quietly on her owner's bed, thinking. She felt cozy on the blue comforter that embraced her like an old friend. Her foxlike ears were pricked at attention as she lay there, her paws crossed in front of her. She watched as the brown tabby cat slowly stretched below her.

Part of Tosha's instinct was to chase the cat. After all, that's what dogs do. But another part of her instinct reminded her that the cat was as big as Tosha.

The cat looked up and mewed. Tosha yawned and lay her head back down on the comforter, snuggling deep within the folds. Too much work, Tosha decided.

Study the Situation Thoroughly

Razor the Husky considered the fence along the back-yard. Surely there was a way out. He poked his nose along the fencing, analyzing it for any weaknesses. He tested the fencing to see if there was a weakness he hadn't seen. He tried digging a bit, here, there. Always testing.

He stood back and looked at the fence. It was six-foot-high chain link. When he was a younger pup, he was able to sail over it. He might be able to climb it now, but he was getting older. Older and

less certain of himself. He hopped on the doghouse and put his paws up on the chain link. Maybe he could just slip over from here?

He put his paws up on the chain link when he heard, "Ack! No!" Razor hopped down to see his owner with her hands on her hips. Foiled again!

Teamwork Is Important

The image of the lone wolf is a fantasy, not a fact. In a wolf pack, the pack relies on every one of the members to do their fair share in the hunt. The alpha wolves (the ones at the top of the pack hierarchy) may lead the hunt, but the other wolves are just as important.

A single wolf may have trouble taking down a bull elk or moose, but several wolves can. Wolves—and dogs—understand the importance of teamwork. Often, wolves take turns chasing down prey to wear it down, so at least one wolf isn't exhausted by the time the prey is. Often there are ambush wolves who drive the prey toward the chase wolves.

After 20,000 years of domestication, dogs still rely on teamwork. In sled teams, the lead dog isn't the only one on the team, and he usually can't pull the sled by himself. He relies on the other dogs to do their part. He may know the way, but he's encouraged by the point dogs, who are right behind him. Behind the point dogs are the swing dogs, who add their muscle and power. Finally, the wheel dogs steer the sled and help keep control of things.

When your dog looks at you with loving eyes, he's looking at you as the leader of a very special team: his team and your team. He will follow where you lead.

Don't Back Bite

Mirin glared at Kiana. The little Husky mix was challenging the Malamute once again. Kiana flashed her teeth at Mirin, who slunk up the stairs. Conan, Cuawn, and Shadow looked from one to the other and then to me. There was dissention in the household.

Like people, sometimes dogs just won't get along, no matter what you try. Kiana found Mirin to be pushy and rude; Mirin thought Kiana was mean-spirited. No matter how hard I tried, the two wound up fighting.

Spaying both dogs and keeping them separated made a huge difference and lowered the tension in the household. But there was always an underlying tension between both females that never was an issue with any of the male dogs. Perhaps the male dogs had come to the conclusion that there was no sense in backbiting.

> **Haegl says . . .**
>
> Arguments about pack hierarchy are common when you add new dogs or when a puppy grows into adolescence. Sometimes the only way to keep the peace between two dogs is to keep them separated.

5

Party Animals

Whether it's a walk in the forest or a game of catch, dogs know that play is very important for both their mental and physical health. In canines, play actually conditions their body and helps them develop their survival skills. When puppies play-wrestle, they learn where to bite effectively. They run to strengthen muscles and joints that could later aid them in chasing down prey. When stalking an unsuspecting littermate, a puppy learns how to hunt. Wrestling prepares the puppy to establish his place in the pack, and playing socializes him with other pack members. Without play, a puppy wouldn't be fit enough to become an efficient pack member.

Our dogs no longer run in wild packs, but they still need—and love—plenty of play, whether it's doing the work they were born to do, playing with toys, or chasing a Frisbee.

With play also comes learning. Some dogs learn by observation, and this, too, is a form of play.

So don't groan when your dog brings you his tennis ball. He's only doing what's natural. And he knows it's good for you, too.

Never Miss a Moment to Be Silly

*P*arty hardy! That's Cinnamon, Audrey, and Ginger's motto. Always looking for fun, these dogs know how to have a good time. Whether it's wearing rabbit ears or romping around the yard in a delicious game of chase, having fun is what every dog knows and does well.

> ### Ranger says . . .
> Be careful with costumes and dogs. Don't leave a dog unattended in a costume and make sure the costume won't overheat the dog or restrict his breathing.

Humans are way too serious. Dogs, on the other hand, know how to let go and have fun for the sake of fun. You wouldn't be caught dead in rabbit ears? Why not?

Always Take Time to Play

Clio the Border Collie was walking with her owner when she saw something beige lying in the grass. Her owner was agitated—obviously in a hurry to get someplace—but Clio just could not pass by the beige thing in the grass.

What was it? Clio wondered. As she approached the object, she could see it was a Frisbee. She first pawed at it, then carefully picked it up in her teeth.

"Here, Clio!" her owner called.

Clio trotted to her owner, Frisbee in her mouth. She deposited it on the grass and looked up at him expectantly. "Clio, we don't have time. . ." the man began.

Clio whined and looked into her owner's eyes with her own soulful brown eyes. "You're always in a hurry," Clio said with her eyes. "You need to have fun."

Her owner smiled as Clio wagged her tail. He picked up the Frisbee and made it sail across the park. Clio leaped after it—she was a blur of black and white. The Frisbee flew just out of the reach of her jaws and slid along the ground, before catching an edge and rolling in a circle. Clio slapped it with her paw and it bounced neatly into her jaws.

She turned back to her owner, who was clapping and laughing. Clio held her tail high as she retrieved the Frisbee for another toss. Her owner sent it sailing high over her, but Clio was ready. She leaped into the air and, with a twist, caught the Frisbee, landed in a full lope, and ran toward her owner.

> **Kira says . . .**
>
> Play is a great stress reliever for humans and dogs. When you're training a dog, always remember to play afterward. It ends the session on a positive note.

With each toss, Clio brought the Frisbee back until she was tired and breathless. Then she sat with her owner and received a big hug for reminding a busy man that no matter how busy you are, there's always time to play.

Have a Sense of Humor

*S*ome experts say dogs can't experience complex emotions, but every dog owner knows this isn't true. I've seen very complex emotions, including humor, in dogs. In fact, Kiana had the most developed sense of humor of any creature I've ever known—dog or otherwise.

Kiana and I always played jokes on each other. One day when she was young, I looked up at the ceiling. Naturally, she looked up. I caught her doing it and laughed and laughed. Kiana made a face, squinting her eyes at me with reproach. She knew I had gotten her good. Sometimes while watching television she'd catch me looking up at the ceiling and sneak a peak, only to find me laughing at her again.

Then one day I was sitting on the couch and Kiana looked up at the ceiling. Not thinking, I looked up and saw nothing. When I looked back at her, she waggled her head from side to side, the way I do when I laugh, her golden eyes gleaming with amusement.

After this, I realized I had created a monster. Kiana would look up at the strangest times and laugh at me when I looked. I had become the victim of my own joke!

Then one day, she looked up. Sure she was planning a joke, I refused to look up. She looked up and then back at me. I didn't look. She looked up again. "Not going to work," I told her.

That's when the spider landed on my head.

Sharing Makes Games More Fun

I tossed the Frisbee, making it soar high above the dogs' heads. Mirin leaped first and was quick to grab the flying disc and race around the yard with it. Then Dancer the Husky chased after her. Together, they played a game of keep-away. Dancer leaped at the Frisbee and Mirin leaped away. Then Mirin paused and held the prize enticingly in a play bow.

Cuawn watched the two carefully. As Mirin skipped just out of Dancer's reach, Cuawn leaped in and grasped the Frisbee as he ran by. Now he had the Frisbee and the other two dogs started chasing him. When he finally let Mirin grab the Frisbee back, his tongue was lolling to one side; Dancer and Mirin played tug-of-war before finally flopping down beside Cuawn. They were all grinning.

She Who Has the Most Toys Wins

Sasha the Golden Retriever stared at the new puppy in the house. Millie, a black Belgian Sheepdog, was chewing on a rubber bone, wagging her tail mischievously.

Sasha grumbled. Those were *her* toys. She picked another bone out of the box and lay down to chew it when Millie came over to

investigate. Sasha leaped up and snatched the pup's rubber bone, so now she had both. Millie whined and went to the toy box and picked out a chew toy. Sasha wandered over, took the chew, and deposited it on her pile.

> **Kodiak says . . .**
>
> It's natural for dogs to try to steal other dogs' toys. As the leader of your pack, you need to enforce the rules of the house and not let any dog bully anyone else too much.

Millie took another toy. Sasha took it away. It continued like this for some time.

Their owner came in to see the pile of toys with Sasha. "Sasha, you naughty girl!" she said as she picked up the toys, handed Millie back her rubber bone, and gave Sasha an identical toy. "Don't be greedy!"

"Nonsense!" Sasha seemed to say. She chewed the rubber bone half-heartedly, keeping a close eye on the puppy. She'd steal back all the toys as soon as her owner wasn't watching. After all, that was the name of the game.

Every Day Is a Good Day to Play

One of the things we love about our canine companions is their desire to play. Regardless of what mood you're in, you can be sure you've always got a willing play partner. Throw a stick. Toss a

ball. Run around the yard and look silly. Your neighbors might point and laugh, but your dog is right beside you all the way.

Your dog knows how stressful your life is. Don't believe me? Watch what he does the next time you've had a bad day. Does he wag his tail as it's tucked between his legs? Does he come over and paw you? Does he clown around and try to make you laugh?

Your dog knows you need to play. Something in our culture has taken the joy out of having fun for fun's sake.

Never Miss an Opportunity for a Morning Walk

The air is crisp with the scent of autumn. The mountain breeze carries a hint of the change in season that comes with cooler mornings. The aspen have started turning their brilliant gold among the pines and conifers. A chipmunk scurries across the path, collecting seeds for the upcoming winter.

Haegl stares in wonder at the beauty before him. The Alaskan Malamute loves to look out over the sunny mountain range and breathe in the cool air. He holds his tail high like a plume as he walks along. He leads his human over rocks to catch sight of the spring fawns and their mother. They've lost their spots now and are watching the Malamute and his owner with cautious curiosity before bounding away to the safety of the ridge.

Haegl sniffs the air and catches the scent of a wood stove. As they continue to walk, he sees the last of the summer wildflowers, red and blue, peeking between the golden aspen leaves on the path. A black bear has eaten the last of the raspberries and gooseberries in preparation for winter. Haegl notices each of these things and many more.

As he and his owner return to their home, Haegl pauses to listen to the chattering stream below. The day becomes so much brighter after a morning walk.

Don't Be Afraid to Step Outside the Rules

I stood nervously at the starting line of the agility course. It was Kiana's and my first venture into the open class, after having gotten our Novice Agility title. Another dog was ahead of us—a German Shepherd.

The agility trial was being held in a musty old horse arena. Typically, trials are held either outdoors or inside horse arenas or barns that are big enough to lay out one or two agility courses. We had come early and staked out our little bit of turf where I could put Kiana's crate. Dust was everywhere.

Dogs have an uncanny knack of knowing your feelings, and Kiana was as good as they came. We watched the team ahead us. The Shepherd went over the jumps, across the dog walk, through the red and blue tunnels, and over the triple jump. I watched carefully. We were just as good—we just didn't need to screw up.

And then it was our turn. I started out pointing to the two jumps. Kiana leaped over each and followed my lead to the dog walk. Next, we took the tunnels and then faced the triple jump. Kiana saw the jump, turned, and went back to the dog walk.

I stared. She refused an obstacle and went off course. We had no chance of redeeming ourselves, but I decided to have her try the triple jump again, anyway. Kiana wagged her head and took the dog walk. Seconds were ticking away.

"Over!" I said and Kiana took the dog walk. Everyone watching burst into laugher, including the judge. The judge blew the whistle, signaling us to leave the course.

Kiana wagged her head at me. She didn't want to do the boring jump—she wanted to do something fun!

Learn by Watching

*H*aegl rang the bell hanging from the doorknob to signal he wanted to go out. It was a small bell suspended from an old leash—just long enough so Haegl could tap it with his paw or nose it.

Kira, an older Malamute, saw Haegl ring the bell and watched as her human let him outside. She studied the bell intently. It hadn't always been there. In fact, it had only been there since Haegl's arrival. She sniffed it and then walked away.

The next time Haegl needed to go out, he rang the bell. Kira went out with him, her mind churning on the bell and its potential. She came back inside and stared at the bell. What if *she* rang it?

Kira gently nosed the bell. It had a metallic scent to it—something dogs don't like—but she had to test her theory. It made no noise. She paused and waited. Then she nosed it again. The faintest tinkle came from the bell and she waited. Her human came and stared.

"Kira, you want to go out?"

Kira wagged her tail. Her human opened the door and Kira walked out into the sunshine.

Invent a New Game

Seizer, a two-year-old Great Dane, was chewing his bone and noticed it moved as he chewed it. So he pushed on it with his paw and the bone skittered across the floor. He jumped after the bone and, as he pushed it on the linoleum floor, it moved again.

Seizer grinned with a big doggy smile. He pushed hard and the bone started moving across the floor. His back legs were on the floor, but he was now surfing with his front paws on the bone.

Myrna, his owner, laughed, watching the antics of her Great Dane as he tried to hang ten on the kitchen floor. The next day, she presented Seizer with a new toy—a skateboard.

It didn't take long for Seizer to learn to slide like a seasoned teenager. He put his front paws on top of the skateboard and pushed himself around, scooting across the linoleum and wooden floors. Then, finally, Seizer got bored and lay down to chew on the board for awhile.

It doesn't take much to invent a new game. Seizer is still having fun hanging ten in New York.

You Don't Have to Win to Have Fun

I stood on the sled runners with my husband Larry's dog team. Cuawn was in the lead next to Kiana. Winnie and her father, the Mighty Quinn, were behind them in the wheel position—the position right in front of the sled. They were big compared to the two dogs in front—a massive pulling force of gray.

It was a bright, warm day in the mountains of Colorado. The sun beat down relentlessly on the snow, making it a blinding white. The air was filled with the cacophony of barking dogs. Teams were pulling and lunging to go. I was holding back the dogs with little success—Malamutes are so powerful that if they want to go someplace, they will.

We were one of the few Alaskan Malamute teams running in this race. I was running Larry's team because he had to work that day. We waited in line to go on our sprint run—four miles across the frozen Lake Dillon.

Before we knew it, we were in the starting chute awaiting our turn. We heard the timers call out to the team in front of us to go and my team lunged forward. I dug the brake into the snow and held on tightly. The timer said something to me, but it was lost above the din. Helpers were hanging onto my sled to hold the team back. I wondered if they could.

Five, four, three, two, one!

Time seems to stand still in the brief moment when the sled dog team leaves the starting chute in a race. Everything slows down as your body pumps adrenaline through your veins. The wild frenzy, the barking, the mad and joyous confusion takes on a surrealistic quality. There is nothing but you, the dogs, and the snow-covered trail now.

I don't have to scream "hike!" The dogs feel the tension release from the brake as I let up. We launch. The noise suddenly abates. We are silent. We fly.

I am part of the team. I think as they do. We must run as a pack. Here we are equals. Yes, I am the ultimate leader, but only because the team wills it. I crouch, gripping the driving bow a little too tightly as the sled careens around a corner. Like a frightened yearling too afraid to stretch out on the racetrack. I chide myself. I try to relax.

The snow is soft and mushy. The temperature is already a little too warm. I can hear the dogs' panting keeping time with the pounding in my ears. The first mile is flat, frozen lake. Then we go uphill onto a little island. The Malamutes don't hesitate. With all that power they take us up and over. We wind through the woods until we break out into the open again. I relax my grip a little.

I am hot and sweating. We take a turn and I lean hard to warp the sled for the turn. Drag a foot into the corner, set up the line, warp tight at the apex of the turn, and use my foot to pedal against the snow to bring the sled around. Do it all over again at the next turn.

Pedal. Pedal. Pedal. Up a hill. Drag feet. Down a hill. There is no real need for commands here—this is sprint racing. We just follow a trail.

We enter the timber again. I see another four-dog team—Siberian Huskies—on the outward-bound trail that runs close to the inward-bound trail. We wave as we pass.

Heading downhill, the Malamutes' tails are high and the dogs are happy. Another team passes us—and yet another. Each team causes my dogs to go into a fast lope before settling down into their typical trot. As we approach the finish line, I can see Kiana and Winnie laughing with joy. Quinn is cheery and happy. Cuawn, constantly devoted to his duty, wags his stub tail. We cross the finish line to clapping and cheering. Last place perhaps, but we sure had a great race!

6
Tail Wags

When it comes to friendship, you'll never find a truer friend than the dog. He can be your confidant and your shoulder to cry on, and he enjoys listening to you even if you aren't a genius or particularly good at conversation. He's always happy to see you and always in a good mood, even if you aren't. He's ready for fun at a moment's notice and he won't let you down. What more could you ask of any friend?

The dog has often been referred to as "man's best friend," and he is humanity's oldest friend, too. Genetics and archaeological records suggest that dogs were probably our first domesticated animals, although there are arguments as to how long ago dogs were domesticated (somewhere between 125,000 and 20,000 years ago is the current best estimate).

Before and throughout civilization, dogs have been with us. First as hunting companions and later bred to guard herds and flocks, pull sleds, and even guard our homes, dogs have been right beside us. They are willing workers and wise companions.

Enjoy Each Other's Company

It was another road trip for the Huskies; this time they were going to Idaho for a race. Tasha sat in her dog box on the truck waiting for Ed. They had known each other their whole lives, running on the team together as mates and as lead dogs. They were both old now. Tasha had long since been retired and Ed had retired recently. They were now together not as race participants, but as observers.

Ed stood on his hind legs and put his paws up on the dog box, waiting for me to lift him up into the box beside Tasha. His brown muzzle was now a faded gray. Tasha peeked out at him to give his

nose a lick before I lifted him into the box. He climbed in—the box already warm with straw and the heat from Tasha's body—and curled around her.

As I closed the door, I smiled. They had enjoyed each other's company throughout their lives and now took comfort in each other in their old age.

Bark before You Bite

Have you ever wondered why dogs bark a lot? Barking can mean many things, including "I'm happy to see you," "Hey, I know you!" "What are you doing here?" and "Keep out! You're scary!" My dogs often bark when they're mad at another dog. I can see them raise their hackles, bark, or growl before they do anything else. Their message is clear: "Stop it! I don't like what you're doing." It's a warning, so there doesn't have to be a fight.

Dogs seldom bite without first giving a warning. It can be a bark, a growl, a snarl, or even standing stiffed-legged and raising the hackles.

Maybe you're angry at a friend, spouse, significant other, or child. Before you "bite," have you given a warning "bark"? Sometimes people don't know that what they're doing is making you angry. Warn them with a "bark" or a "growl"; you don't want a fight. Give them a chance to stop before you sink your teeth into them.

Be There for Your Friends

The two Malamute puppies were gone.

My stomach churned as I looked at the downed chain-link fence. That night we got plenty of heavy, wet snow, typical for early spring in the Rocky Mountains. The heavy snow snapped branches, whole trees, power lines—and my backyard fence. And that fence was the only barrier between Kira and Kodiak, my seven-month-old puppies, and the wilderness.

Ranger was gone too. The gangly German Shepherd was nowhere in sight. Instead, tracks crisscrossed and led down to the creek, through thick brush, and into the valley that led toward miles of national forest.

People lose dogs and cats all the time in the mountains. Many are never recovered; they die of starvation or fall prey to cougars and bears. I ran into the knee-deep snow calling for the puppies. My husband, Larry, donned his boots and parka. He followed the tracks, but they went everywhere—he could chase a dozen false trails and not find the dogs.

Meanwhile, halfway around the mountain, the two Malamute puppies frolicked in the snow while Ranger watched nervously. Then he heard it—someone calling his name. He nudged the puppies forward, following my voice.

I spotted movement. "Ranger!" I screamed, my voice hoarse from yelling. "Ranger brought back the puppies!"

Larry climbed through the deep snow and brambles. He found a very relieved Ranger and a joyful Kira, but no Kodiak.

"Where's Kodiak?" he asked the two dogs. They led him nearly half a mile before finding Kodiak perched above a ravine. The puppy was ready to bolt.

"Ranger, go get Kodiak!" Larry ordered.

Without hesitation, Ranger headed straight for the puppy. He batted the puppy's muzzle with his paw. Kodiak jumped and Ranger nipped, driving the puppy toward Larry. Larry snapped leashes on the puppies and walked them both home. Ranger calmly walked beside them like the hero he was.

Set an Example

The Alaskan Husky grins impishly as he watches the other dogs get loaded up into the dog truck. "Take me! Take me!" he barks insistently. He knows he's too old to run now—his glory days are long gone—but he still likes hanging around the sled team. At thirteen years old, Ed enjoys going on long trips with the team—like some old codger sitting on the porch watching the young whippersnappers in a sport that he excelled at in his heyday. Perhaps he offers sage advice to the younger lead dogs that took his place a few years ago, when arthritis forced him to retire.

We go on walks frequently. I snap the leash on Ed's flat collar and we do a kind of puppy dance. He spins around me like a whirligig, hopelessly tangling me in the leash. "What's over here? What's over there?" he seems to ask as he sees something that catches his interest. I hop over the leash— jump rope with a Husky! I gently call to him and he bounds into my arms—sixty pounds of wriggling thirteen-year-old puppy.

He's a homely thing to look at. He doesn't look like a Husky—the short black and tan coat, the barely furred rattail, the ears that flop to the side but prick up when something interests him. It's hard to believe he comes from top racing lines. Even in the prime of his life he could have been mistaken for a junkyard dog or a stray mutt. But when I look at him, all I see is the big heart behind the slightly clouded eyes.

Be Loyal to the End

Conan had stopped eating. The old dog was getting emaciated as cancer began to eat at his body. He took to lying outside in the sun, waiting for the inevitable.

Cuawn lay quietly next to him. The Australian Shepherd was concerned for his buddy. They had grown up together and had been inseparable. Now, as disease was ready to close Conan's eyes, Cuawn had one last gift to give: companionship.

Conan died at thirteen years old. Cuawn lived four more years after that. Often, I think he would lie down and think about his old friend.

> **Ranger says . . .**
>
> Check your dog over once a week for any health problems and take him to the veterinarian for a checkup at least once a year.

7

Puppy Love

*L*ove. The word is almost synonymous with dogs. The love and faithfulness of a dog knows no bounds. As humans, we've marveled over the dog's love and faithfulness through history. In *The Odyssey*, Homer exalts the dog: When Odysseus comes home after twenty long years, the only one to recognize him is the dog he got as a pup before he left for Troy. That puppy, now an old dog, dies after licking his master's hand.

How often in our lives do we fall short of the pure, complete love of dogs? Dogs love unconditionally and honestly. We admire them for their simple act of love. The world would be a better place if we all learned something about love from our dogs.

Love Doesn't Need Words

Allison stared at the puppies in the shelter. They were all so wiggly and cute. Just about every type of breed and mixed breed was available.

"Which one should we get?" her mother asked.

Allison said nothing. Instead, she saw the little spotted Dalmatian puppy in the corner, huddled by herself. Allison pointed to it and clapped her hands in delight.

"That's a deaf puppy," the shelter worker said. She opened the cage door and picked up the puppy. "She'll have special needs."

"That's okay," said her mother. "So does Allison."

The shelter worker gently picked up the puppy and placed her in Allison's arms. The puppy wriggled, licking Allison's face, and the girl began crying for joy.

Thank you, Allison signed to the shelter worker.

> **Kira says . . .**
>
> Deafness is common in some lines of Dalmatians and Australian Shepherds. These dogs make wonderful pets once their owners learn how to train them using sign language.

Love Unconditionally

illie's eyes were as dark as her fur, black as coal, set into a sweet face. The little Belgian Sheepdog gazed up soulfully into her new owner's eyes and pawed at her gently. Millie

nuzzled Carol. Carol picked her up and cradled her. So much love; so much trust.

When you look into your puppy's eyes, you are her entire world. A puppy knows how special you are regardless of who you are, what you did or didn't do, whether you're pretty or ugly, rich or poor.

Look into a puppy's eyes. There you will find complete love.

Share Your Love with Your Friends

All the dogs gathered at the dog park. First came Buster, a chocolate Labrador Retriever who wags his tail so fiercely you'd think he might smack someone. Next came Sadie, the white Jack Russell Terrier with brown patches, carrying her favorite squeaky toy. Then came Indy, a German Shepherd Dog who loves to play with everyone.

As more dogs gathered, they broke off into groups. Sometimes they romped all over the park, having a great time. Other times, they chased flying discs or tennis balls thrown by their humans.

Rusty wagged his tail nervously. With all these strange dogs, the Golden Retriever wasn't sure what to do. Then, he saw the tennis ball and leaped forward, chasing after the ball before he even knew what he was doing.

He caught the ball and turned around to see Sadie and Buster wagging their tails and keeping their heads lowered in a friendly gesture. They weren't here to fight, they were here to play. Before he knew it, Rusty was making friends. Sadie licked his nose affectionately and Buster gave him a good, hearty thump. Their goodwill quickly got Rusty past his nervousness.

Make Someone Feel Better

The little girl fell off her bike and was crying. Max, a Golden Retriever who lived next door, loped over. At first she stared at him, wiping the tears from her eyes. Max sat down beside her and held out his paw. She took it and he smiled gently. Then Max placed his head on her shoulders as she wrapped her small arms around his neck and slid her fingers into his deep, red-gold fur. He licked her ear gently with his big tongue.

They had seen one another before, but they didn't know each other. The girl leaned in. Max squirmed closer. He was there when she thought no one else cared and lessened her pain.

Love Doesn't Care About Money

*W*ill work for food." The homeless man sat on the street corner with a sign and an empty can. People drove by, oblivious to the man with the dusty coat, worn shoes, salt and pepper hair, and creased face. His dog sat beside him, a little black and gray terrier mix. The dog had a rope that worked for both his collar and leash. The old man held onto him tightly as he shook the can for money.

The dog's soulful eyes looked up at his owner. The old man knelt down, reached into his pocket, and pulled out a greasy hamburger from a fast-food restaurant. He broke the hamburger in two and offered a half to the dog, who gulped it down in two bites.

The old man smiled. Together, they could face anything.

Everyone Needs to Be Loved

"Free dog to good home" read the sign in front of the house. The woman heard Shadow the Keeshond whine as he sat alone in the hot garage on a summer day. She peered in the window. Shadow had plenty of toys and food, but no one to enjoy them with. He took a sip of lukewarm water from his bowl and whined as if to say, "Certainly, someone will play with me soon."

Shadow's owner opened the garage door for the woman and she walked inside. Shadow jumped up, barking with joy at seeing the new person. Shadow threw himself into the woman's open arms, wriggling uncontrollably and licking her face. Then he pulled back and did a little dance on his hind feet, twirling around in joy.

"He's perfect!" she said, burying her face in his warm, gray fur and feeling his tongue as he licked her enthusiastically. Someone cared!

Kiss Everyone

*M*ost dogs are great kissers. They greet new people as if they were long, lost friends and give everyone a thorough face wash when they meet them. It may be annoying to some people, but they aren't dog people. (Why are you associating with them, anyway?) Doesn't it make you feel good when your dog kisses you?

> *Haegl says . . .*
>
> **Socialization is very important for dogs. Whether you have a puppy or an adult, have your dog meet people, visit unfamiliar and exciting places, and play with other dogs. You'll have a well-adjusted pet if you do. One place to go is puppy kindergarten. Most trainers offer this class for young puppies to learn in a controlled environment how *not to* become afraid of other puppies, people, and things.**

My dogs are enthusiastic greeters. They bellow and wag their tails when they see someone new. You're their friend now and they're going to kiss you. Watch out!

Okay, maybe it's not the best idea to kiss *everyone*. But kiss *everyone you know* when you greet them. It'll make them feel special and they'll know they are loved.

Love Is a Gift

Serena was a sable and white Collie. At twelve years old, she was no longer agile; her hips were stiff with arthritis and dysplasia. I grew up with her, and she was my constant companion through elementary, junior, and high school. Now, home from college for Christmas, I looked at my friend in dismay. Cataracts glazed those once bright eyes. Her nose was clogged with strange polyps. She ignored basic commands—a sure sign of deafness.

It was a warm winter afternoon a few days before Christmas. I took her leash—more out of habit, really, since she was trustworthy off leash—and invited her to go for a walk. She rose stiffly from her customary spot beside the couch and walked to the door. Not long ago, Serena had barked happily and dashed around in circles. But the excitement was gone. She stood patiently as I opened the door.

We walked together along the familiar bike path toward the nearby park as I thought back to happier times. I remembered when we first brought her home—an unwanted three-month-old puppy "at a real bargain" from a backyard breeder. To me as a seven year old, she seemed so big. I could not pick her up and cuddle her the way other kids could with their puppies. It didn't really matter though, because I knew I had the most splendid puppy of all.

A smart dog, Serena quickly learned to stay in our yard and not stray—something I would not trust a dog about now. She was always a constant friend and confidant when others failed. She was there to share snacks or play tag or learn a new trick to impress people. She suffered the indignity of being wheeled around in a wheelbarrow by a group of bored kids and performed endless stunts of leaping over hurdles. Tag with her was great fun. She could outrun anyone. She dashed around in circles, laughing at us as we ended up face down in the grass from trying to catch her.

Where was that companion now? This dog hardly resembled the one I grew up with. She plodded along slowly, head lowered, no longer caring what smells enticed her. I wondered if she could even smell. I stopped for a moment and watched her trundle past me, then called to her. She kept walking, not noticing me standing there. *What was wrong with her?* I wondered.

I had changed too. My first year at college, away from home, was a sobering experience. I was struggling in difficult engineering and physics classes and I was homesick. I missed my family and Colorado's beauty. In college, I was more than 500 miles away from the only true friend I had in the world. I was beginning to think going away to college was a mistake.

We stopped near a pond we often walked to. I began petting Serena and telling her what a wonderful dog she was. I knew she couldn't hear me, but somehow talking to her comforted me. I told her all the problems I had at school and how much I missed her. I hugged her as she slowly licked my face. Somehow I knew she understood. The heart does not need hearing, sight, or even smell to understand. I stood up and said, "Come on, Serena, let's play!"

Suddenly, I was no longer eighteen, but seven years old again, and she was six months old instead of twelve years. Serena barked and crouched down, inviting me to play. Forgetting my problems, I chased her in a glorious game of tag. She was still faster than me! She whirled around in circles, laughing at me as we ran through the park. Those eyes dimmed by cataracts shone as bright as a puppy's. Both out of breath, we stopped and hugged. She wriggled in my arms, my old friend again. It would soon be Christmas and I would receive presents, but this was the best present of all—the chance to play with my old friend again. She gave me back something I had lost: the chance to be carefree.

Soon her eyes glazed over and her head lowered again. We walked home in silence and I knew then this was her final gift to me. I would not see her again. Right now, it didn't matter. I was with her and she was with me, as it always had been. We shared a deep understanding. It would be a merry Christmas and one I would remember for a long time.

A month later, I called my parents from college and asked how Serena was doing. "Fine," they told me with an edge in their voices that told me she was not fine. They assured me nothing was wrong. Not long after, I found out Serena had a brain tumor and had to be euthanized. Looking back on that day in the park comforted me greatly. I wished I could have been there to ease her to her journey over the Rainbow Bridge, but somehow she comforted me when I grieved.

I don't believe in ghosts. But sometimes, late at night around Christmas, my eye will catch a movement and I swear I see what looks like a sable and white Collie standing beside me. Perhaps it is just wishful thinking or an overactive imagination, but maybe Serena is still reminding me how strong the human-dog bond really is.

Forgive and Forget

*M*irin shivered in the vet's office. She was a small white mixed breed with upright ears, corkscrew tail, and bright blue eyes that made her look as if she was smiling all the time.

Mirin wasn't smiling now, though. All around her were strange smells and strange dogs. A Schnauzer lay beside his owner, quietly whimpering. A woman sat with a cat carrier and two mewing cats. No one spoke. At another time Mirin might be interested in the cats, but not here. Not now. The place smelled of antiseptic, bleach, and fearful dogs.

After being brought into the exam room, a strange man began poking and prodding her. She glanced apprehensively at her owner, her tail tucked firmly between her legs. One prick of a needle and she yelped, ki-yi-ing as loudly as she could.

The man knelt down. "Sorry about that, sweetheart. Do you want a biscuit?"

Mirin sniffed at the biscuit in his open hand. She glanced at her owner, who nodded. "Go ahead, Mirin."

Gently, Mirin took the biscuit from the man's hand and tentatively wagged her tail. He petted her under the chin and Mirin found her eyes drooping as she pressed her nose into his hand. He gave her neck a good scratch. Soon, all was forgiven—and forgotten.

Protect Those You Love

He's hurt," the woman said as I got out of my car. There were two Labrador Retrievers, one chocolate and one yellow, by the side of the road. The chocolate Lab had obviously been hit by a car. The yellw one stood between the bystanders and his wounded companion. "We've called animal control to help these two guys."

I had dealt with many dogs before. "Hey there, big fella," I said softly to the yellow Lab, avoiding eye contact with the dog. "Let me see your buddy." I crouched down to make myself less threatening.

"Grrrrr," said the yellow Lab. He glanced at his companion, who weakly thumped his tail. The yellow Lab made it crystal clear to me that he would not let me near.

> **Ranger says . . .**
>
> **Dogs aren't smart when it comes to cars—most are just lucky. We're safer and more secure when we're home behind a fence.**

I stood up as the animal control officer arrived. She gently caught the yellow Lab with a noose and led him away before tending to his buddy. "Don't worry," she told the dog, "he'll be all right." She came back for the injured dog and muzzled him before picking him up and taking him to the truck. "He has a broken leg. I've notified a vet near here that I'm bringing him in," she said. "He's got tags. By the looks of it, these guys probably just got out of their yard."

Being in a strange place and injured—it's frightening for any dog. But what impressed me was the yellow dog. That Lab knew his friend was hurt and would protect him at any cost.

Even the Unlovable Need Love

The black and tan German Shepherd was standing alone and forgotten in the middle of the highway. Mud and pine tar encrusted his bedraggled coat, which barely hid his ribs as they made a washboard across his chest. He looked up at the cars as they whizzed by.

Walking slowly, he shied as a car came to a screeching halt in front of him. He jumped and crouched submissively. The car scooted forward and honked again. He sidled to one side. The car sped off, the driver not bothering to notice the pitiful shape he was in.

The German Shepherd felt miserable. Within his gut, parasites sucked away his blood and stole his nutrients. His ears and face were bloody from fly bites; the tips of his ears were gone. At some time he had been chained, but had caught the chain around his back leg and had struggled to get free. He still bore the scars of it. He was twenty pounds underweight.

He made another dash into the road when he heard a friendly voice. "Hey fella! Come here!"

The German Shepherd looked to see a blond man call to him from the side of the road. The dog scuttled toward him just as a car came to a screeching halt and the owner slammed on his horn. For a moment, the dog hesitated, but then he ran to the man, whose arms were outstretched to him.

The dog dropped to the ground and rolled over. "There's a good boy," the man said, stroking him. "Come on, let's get you to safety." The man led the dog to the open door of an SUV. "Come on, good boy. We'll take care of you."

The German Shepherd melted in the man's arms as he helped the dog into the car. At last—a loving home.

Be a Good Listener

Kiana cocked her head to one side as I told her about my day: the idiot bosses, clueless coworkers, the tough schedules ahead. Then, very solemnly, she stared into my face with her golden eyes and gently gave me her paw to hold.

I hugged her, burying my face in her pure white mane. She smiled her doggy smile and laid her head against my shoulders. She understood I was upset and knew I just needed someone to listen.

Greet Your Loved Ones Enthusiastically

*I*t's a beautiful, sunny day and Sadie is lying on the lawn. It's warm outside and she's drowsy. She flicks an annoyed ear at a persistent fly that buzzes around her head. She yawns and lays her head against her paws.

Suddenly, her ears perk up. What's that in the distance? She raises her head to look. A car? But not just any car. Her special person's car.

Sadie is on her feet before she's even thought about it. Her special person is home! She leaps into the air and bounds toward the fence where she'll see her person get out of the car.

The car slows to a stop in the driveway and that special person gets out.

"Sadie!" says her human. "Have you been a good girl?"

Sadie is wiggling all over, her tail slapping rhythmically against her flanks. Of course she has! And now the day is that much better.

8

Family Values

Charles Schultz once said, "Happiness is a warm puppy." It most certainly is. Everyone loves puppies, and there isn't anything cuter. In fact, puppies were born cute so you wouldn't yell at them when they do something wrong.

When you look into those big, trusting eyes, you can't help but be amazed at the world around you. How could something so innocent and loving exist in this world? A puppy makes the world a brighter place.

As a puppy grows and becomes a dog, he needs to learn things. A puppy learns a lot from his mom and his owner. Finding a mentor to teach him the important stuff is also important—as Haegl has done with Quinn.

And yes, puppies can do dastardly deeds! How many chewed-up shoes and unrolled sheets of toilet paper have you found in your house when you had a puppy?

In spite of all that, we still love pups. Their sweet, innocent looks capture our hearts every time.

Set a Good Example

Quinn looked at the puppy. Both were Malamutes, but Haegl was only a few months old and tiny next to Quinn. Quinn was an old Alaskan Malamute, going on thirteen years. Age had caught up to Quinn and arthritis was giving his hips problems. He was on pain medications, and while he still enjoyed walking, the process was becoming more difficult. Now he was looking at the puppy with interest.

It had been years since Quinn had seen a puppy. The puppy looked up at the big dog—Haegl's head could have easily fit inside Quinn's mouth. Haegl licked the big dog's nose and Quinn smiled. Quinn had a job he could still do.

"Come on, kid," Quinn said. "I'll show you the ropes."

As they both started out on their walk, Haegl wanted to bounce around and play. Quinn watched patiently until the puppy had settled down before going into his steady walk. Haegl watched his new friend as Quinn showed him what he needed to know.

"Head lowered and pull," Quinn said. "You'll need to do that when you're in harness with the sled."

> **Haegl says . . .**
>
> Dogs, like humans, learn by watching other dogs. Many dogs learn both good and bad habits this way.

Haegl began to imitate Quinn's stance. Instead of bouncing around, he settled into a lower pulling stance, just like Quinn. Head lowered, he braced himself and began pulling. "Good job," Quinn said.

As they walked by some bushes, Quinn lifted his leg. Haegl paused to sniff and tried to lift his leg too, but was too young to balance. He settled on squatting before taking off after Quinn.

Everything Quinn did, Haegl tried. If Quinn stopped to smell something interesting, Haegl was right there sniffing alongside him. If Quinn marked an object with urine, Haegl tried as well. If Quinn walked a certain way, Haegl did too. Quinn found a young pal who shed some sunshine on the old guy's life. And Haegl found a mentor.

Set Boundaries

ailey stared at the toilet paper on the roll. The Golden Retriever puppy knew he could have fun if he grabbed it. He crept up on it, moving one paw slowly in front of the other. He could do this if he were quick enough.

With a leap, he grabbed the first sheet in his teeth and ran, unrolling the paper behind him. First into the kitchen and then into the living room.

"Bailey!" his owner shouted.

Bailey ran to the family room where his bed was and then looked behind him in surprise. The toilet paper roll had followed him

somehow! He looked down and realized he still had the end in his mouth. He dropped it and curled up into a ball.

"Bailey!" his owner said reproachfully.

Bailey wagged his tail and lowered his head. "Could you really be mad at me?" Bailey asked.

His owner laughed and put up the baby gates. "My fault, Bailey!" she said, rolling up the toilet paper and closing the bathroom door. "I should've kept the gates up."

Correct Gently

"*N*o, Ferdie—outside!"

Ferdie found himself scooped up and traveling through the air. A moment before, he had discovered a nice place to relieve himself on the carpet. Now he found himself outside in the grass, with so many more interesting things to do. He sniffed the grass.

"Go on, Ferdie," his owner said.

Ferdie was confused. He wasn't supposed to relieve himself inside? He walked over the grass and sniffed around. He could smell the earth beneath his feet and the heady aroma of cut bluegrass. There was a bug there, too. He followed the bug with his nose.

But suddenly nature called. Ferdie stopped and relieved himself. "Good Ferdie!" his owner said.

Ferdie looked up, surprised. His owner picked him up again and brought him inside. Lesson learned.

> **Kodiak says...**
>
> To keep Ferdie (and your own dog) from returning to the same inappropriate place for his bathroom, use vinegar and water to hide the scent or a commercial enzymatic cleaner made to clean up dog messes. Don't use ammonia-based products because they enhance the urine smell.

Teach Your Pups What They Need to Know

*T*asha's four puppies played together. Three cute little red balls of fur and one gray one, they tussled and tumbled about. Tasha watched.

Whenever they got too rough or bossy toward one puppy, she would step in and place her slender muzzle between theirs and the puppy they were picking on. When

> *Kira says ...*
>
> **Puppies need to be with mom until they're at least eight weeks old. Otherwise, they don't learn some very important life lessons from her.**

they ate, Tasha would eat and then watch to make sure each puppy ate well. Each time they played, Tasha made certain each puppy knew his place and how to interact with the others.

Tasha was teaching them to be good dogs—something every puppy must learn.

Comfort a Frightened Pup

Haegl was eight weeks old and had never seen anything so terrible in his life. He stared at the creature in front of him. It was huge—larger than he was. It was tawny, with black and orange. And it wasn't dog or human. He ki-yied pitifully and ran behind my legs.

The creature gazed at him with slitted green eyes and moved away. Haegl watched it fearfully.

"It's okay," I said, picking him up and holding him close. "It's just Hailey the cat."

Haegl wuffed softly and pressed his head into my arms.

Protect Your Pups

Chloe, a tricolor Dachshund, nuzzled the two black pups who nursed against her. She rested her chin lightly on the pups and coiled her long body as tight as it would go. Unless one looked closely, one might simply think Chloe was napping.

Louie the red Dachshund walked into the room and stopped. Chloe lifted her head and fixed him with a stare. Louie wagged his tail and lowered his head. Didn't Chloe want to play?

> **Kira says . . .**
>
> Make your dog feel special. You can make special treats for your dog right in your own kitchen. Maggie has some wonderful treat recipes in the appendix.

A low growl issued from Chloe's throat. "Stay away!" she said in an unmistakable tone.

"Come on, Louie!" Louie heard his owner call. "Leave Chloe alone—she has work to do. Want to play fetch?"

Louie turned and waddled away. Fetch sounded like a great idea.

Provide a Safe Place for Your Pups

*S*amantha, a Samoyed, looked over the windswept prairie. She was searching. She was looking for a special safe place. Someplace warm, cozy, and safe. But since she was an indoor dog, she couldn't find such a place.

The prairie was full of coyotes, foxes, and even the occasional mountain lion. Hawks and eagles flew overhead and rattlesnakes abounded. There was little cover except the scrub oak and knotty pines that occasionally dotted the land. Mostly there was sage, tumbleweeds, and pampas grass. This was not a safe place.

> *Ranger says...*
>
> **About 5 million animals are put to death in shelters each year; many are purebred dogs. Spay or neuter your pet!**

Samantha had tried to tell her owners several times how important it was to find this safe place, but they didn't understand. So she went off on her own to find it. She found the remains of a prairie dog hole and began digging. She dug and dug. Then she waited. She knew it was time.

In the morning, there were six healthy puppies nursing from her: four white, one black, and one black and white. Samantha hoped her owners would find her soon.

When You're Scolded, Look Hurt

"Bad dog!" I said pointing to the chewed-up papers. Cuawn met my gaze with large, soulful, brown eyes. He squeaked a little, dropping the paper from his mouth.

I grasped the paper and brandished it at him. "Look what you did!"

He continued looking at me with those soulful eyes and cowered a bit.

"Cuawn, I . . ." And then I shut up and I whisked him into my arms. Dog:1; Human: 0.

A Tired Puppy Is a Happy Puppy

At nearly 10,000 feet above sea level, 60 degrees feels blistering hot. The sun is brighter and the sky takes on a deep, tranquil blue. Winnie the Malamute stands in a field of wildflowers, breathing air untouched by pollution and humidity. She overlooks the Continental Divide where the Rocky Mountains touch the sky at over 14,000 feet. It's early July and the snowline has receded, but there are still pockets of sugar snow hiding in the shade of aspens and coniferous trees.

Winnie has carried the pack up the hill. Beside her is her dad, Quinn, and her cousin Boots. Each of them carries packs, too. It's a long hike—ten miles—but they don't feel it now. They're having too much fun out here.

On returning, Winnie falls asleep next to her dad in the car. A fun day out makes for a tired pup.

> ## *Haegl says . . .*
>
> Backpacking with a dog is great fun, but always have a veterinarian check your dog before you begin any type of activity. On the first few hikes, load the dog with only 5 percent of his own weight, and slowly increase the load as the dog becomes accustomed to it. Most breeds can handle 15 to 20 percent of their weight—healthy Malamutes can carry a full 30 percent.

9

Stay Healthy

All dogs—with some warped exceptions—hate visiting the vet. It usually ranks right up there with baths and toenail trimmings. The smells of sickness, the whining animals, the disinfectant—and, of course, the vaccinations and surgery—leave even the most macho dogs pleading for their lives.

The fact is, you can make visits to the vet a happier experience. Every now and then, bring your dog to the vet's office for a quick cookie and to say hi to the staff. A few quick and fun visits to the vet, followed by visits to the dog park, will help every dog get over his terror of the vet's office.

You can also reduce vet visits by practicing basic preventive care. Keep your dog brushed and free of mats, clean his ears, brush his teeth, and examine him weekly for lumps, bumps, and potential health problems.

Avoid the Vet If You Can

*T*eddy shivered violently and crouched low as his owner brought him in. Teddy knew exactly where he was. The smell of sickness and fear lingered over the scent of bleach and disinfectant.

Teddy looked from dog to dog as they sat in the waiting room. A Sheltie was barking at Teddy, trying to get his attention. A Rottweiler puppy had his leash in his mouth and was playing tug-of-war with his owner. Teddy heard mewing beside him and cocked his head. Next to his owner sat a woman with a bag that was obviously making that noise. A few sniffs convinced Teddy there was a cat in the bag.

"Teddy?"

Teddy looked up and his owner led him to an exam room. Teddy tried to pull away, but to no avail. He knew he was doomed. The man in the white coat would stick him with needles and poke and prod him all over. No matter how nice the man was and no matter how well Teddy behaved, the dog knew this was going to hurt.

Get Plenty of Exercise

Maggie, a dark German Shorthaired Pointer mix, watched the squirrel as it ran up the tree in her backyard. She ran and tried to catch it, barking wildly. The squirrel looked down, chittered his annoyance, and flicked his tail at her. Maggie put her paws on the tree trunk and barked, "Come down!" The squirrel moved to a higher branch.

At that moment, Maggie caught movement out of the corner of her eye. Another squirrel! This time a red one. Maggie lunged at the red squirrel, barking. This squirrel didn't run to the nearest tree, but instead ran across the yard to the fence. Maggie rushed after him, loping as fast as her spotted paws would go. This time she'd catch that squirrel!

Drink Lots of Water

Everyone knows they should drink water when it's hot outside. But what about when it's cold? Working dogs like Buddy, an Alaskan Malamute, need as much water when it's cold as when it's hot. The cold air dries their skin out but, because they're not hot, they sometimes forget to drink.

> **Kira says . . .**
>
> Dehydration is serious business and can be fatal. Always provide water from a known, clean water source and make sure your dog gets plenty of it.

Buddy loves a warm soupy broth of meat scraps and water. It tastes good and gets water into his parched body. Just a little dehydration can make a huge difference in a dog's performance. So whether he's weight pulling, sledding, or skijoring, Buddy's owner, Charlene LaBelle, keeps him well hydrated and ready to do whatever is ahead.

Keep Your Teeth Clean

Chop-Chop, a red Chow Chow, holds the big knuckle bone between his paws and gnaws on it. He can taste the little bit of meat on it, and the chewing action works his gums so he has healthy teeth.

Dogs are natural chewers. Most large dogs have enough strength in their jaws to create about 400 pounds of biting force. Those jaws can tear muscle, crack bone, and rip through the toughest hide. But, like us, dogs can have problems with their teeth. Chewing bones helps prevent these problems.

Ranger says . . .

Don't use human toothpaste to brush teeth, because the fluoride is poisonous to dogs. Use toothpaste made for dogs.

So does a little help from his owner, who brushes Chop-Chop's teeth so he can enjoy a healthy set of teeth into his senior years.

Eat a Well-Balanced Diet

*R*obyn, the Cocker Spaniel–Golden Retriever mix, thinks ice cream is one of the basic food groups. While snacks are indeed important, Robyn also gets a diet that's formulated for dogs with high-quality protein.

Like people, dogs suffer from obesity. Doling out snacks, table scraps, and other tidbits isn't healthy for dogs any more than it is healthy for humans. And while our canine friends will eat darn near anything, not everything is good for them. Your dog will live longer—and so will you—with a proper diet.

Kira says . . .

Plain, canned pumpkin makes a delicious low-calorie treat any dog will love.

Keep Active to Stay Young

The sled team was barking and lunging against the gangline again. Houston and Cheyenne were in the lead position, followed by Razor in point, and finally Miki and Panda in wheel. I had stopped the sled for them to rest, but now they wanted to go again.

I set the snowhooks in the hard pack snow and left the runners to give each of them a pat and a rub behind the ears. Panda and Miki were first. I had rescued them from a shelter. Panda was a pretty, gray girl with markings like goggles and large eyes that were slightly cross-eyed. She melted into my hand as I petted her. Miki did a little dance with his front feet as I turned to him and rubbed his ears. A gray and white dog, he almost looked like a coyote with his long legs.

Next came Razor, gray showing on his muzzle as he turned to me. Razor was all white except for his red-brown head and black spots on his body. He leaned into me as I petted him.

> ## Kodiak says . . .
>
> **Start slow in any exercise regimen. Begin with short walks or jogs and playing fetch or Frisbee, and work your way up. If your dog is out of condition, consult your vet for a diet to help shed those extra pounds and to make sure your dog has no underlying health problems.**

I went to my lead dogs last. Cheyenne, my little lead dog, is maybe thirty-five pounds and is all white. She tippy-toed onto her hind legs to give me a kiss. Houston, my black and tan dog, looks more like a Beagle than a lead dog. He wagged his tail and leaned forward, ready to go at my command.

As I walked back to the sled, I took a look at my motley crew. Some of them, like Cheyenne, I've raised from puppies. Others I've gotten along the way. They were excited and ready to go. They were also all over nine years old.

They're not fast, but they run well. Some dogs, like Houston, are getting too old to pull anymore, but he'll keep trying until he can't. Some of my dogs have been in my team until they were thirteen years old and have lived to seventeen or better.

As I pulled the snowhooks and gave them the command to run again, I wondered if I had found the fountain of youth. Staying active has made for some long-lived Huskies.

Tell Someone When You're Sick

Razor stared at his food and then back at me. Something was wrong. The Alaskan Husky normally ate his food, but now he picked at it. He'd taste a little and then stare at it as if he wanted to eat but just couldn't.

Razor was a healthy Husky even though he was eleven years old. Physically fit, he still ran on my sled team. It wasn't like him to just stop eating. A day passed and then another. Instead of eating his food, Razor cached it in a hole he dug and then covered with dirt.

Dogs who are good eaters don't just stop eating. It's their way of telling you something is definitely wrong. I looked Razor over but could find nothing. He was healthy and fit. Then I opened his mouth and, to my surprise, saw a growth behind his front canines. I took Razor to the vet, who found five benign tumors in Razor's mouth and removed them. Razor was so relieved the first night back home that he ate all his food.

Don't suffer in silence. Tell someone you're sick.

> **Ranger says . . .**
>
> Examine you dog once a week from head to toe—including inside his mouth.

Have a Pet

*H*aegl bellowed at the top of his lungs. He was standing at the fence looking at the creature on the ground. It was a small bull snake, still lethargic in the early morning. Haegl stared at the little black snake as it flicked its tongue toward him. Harmless bull snakes abound in the Rocky Mountains and eat rodents.

Haegl was bemused. What was this odd creature? It was unlike anything he had seen before. As the snake woke, it moved toward Haegl and Haegl crooned at it. A new friend? Maybe a pet? He put out his paw to try to touch the snake, but the fence prevented it. He continued to watch the snake as it slithered toward its hole.

Later that afternoon, Haegl was outside again and saw the snake. He sat down now and watched it, completely fascinated. The snake sunned itself and Haegl spoke to it with deep woo-woos. It seemed to work for them both.

Throughout the summer, Haegl would get up and go outside to look for his pet snake. At last, when the nights started getting too cold, the snake moved off to lower elevations or perhaps even hibernated. Haegl continued to look for his pet snake, but in vain.

Winter came and passed and Haegl had forgotten about his pet, until one spring day when he walked outside and saw the little black snake lying just outside the fence. He woo-wooed his greeting, ecstatic to find his pet snake again.

Buckle Up

Sadie closed her eyes as the car's movement gently rocked her to sleep. The miles slipped away and the warm sun on her back made her drowsy. She was comfy here—not outside in a truck bed, exposed to the elements. Inside and buckled up with a special canine seatbelt, she wouldn't have to try to hang on if there was a sudden stop. She was secure.

> *Haegl says . . .*
>
> **If your dogs are too squirmy for a seatbelt, try crating them in the back of the car. Never let your dog ride outside a crate in a truck bed and never leave a dog alone in the car on a warm, sunny day.**

Keep Your Wounds Clean

How many times have you seen a dog lick a wound? It's a natural instinct for dogs to keep their wounds clean, because in the wild there are plenty of germs that can cause an infection. But is it true that a dog's mouth is cleaner than a human's?

Dog saliva is no cleaner than human saliva and it doesn't have healing properties. In fact, dog saliva actually has enzymes that dissolve flesh. Anyone who has suffered a dog bite knows firsthand how quickly a bite wound can become infected. But when you're faced with a dirty wound or a wound that's cleaned up with a lick, the cleaned-up wound is always better.

But as any pet owner whose dog had to wear an Elizabethan collar will tell you, veterinarians don't like dogs worrying at their bandages or wounds. Keep your wounds clean. Dogs know to do this instinctively, even if their methods are less than perfect.

Know When to Let Go

*L*et her go, Maggie."

I was crying and barely coherent as I heard the words of truth from my longtime veterinarian, who was on the phone. Spice, my white Alaskan Husky, was dying. She was suffering from a condition called DIC, where the body simply shuts down. Spice had begun to bleed internally, and she was at the emergency room. I had spent thousands of dollars on her care already and was unemployed. The prognosis was not good and my vet was being honest with me.

"It's time to let her go, Maggie," he said. "She won't live forever and I told you when we last talked that she probably wouldn't make it."

I was feeling alone in the emergency room. The vets there were expecting me to continue putting Spice through this ordeal. She was gray from loss of blood and was on a respirator. Tubes snaked in and out of her in every direction. She looked into my eyes and told me plainly, "End this now."

My vet was the voice of reason in this. I thanked him and hung up the phone. My husband, Larry, was waiting for me to tell him what we were going to do. "The vet says we should let her go."

I held Spice in my arms and wept as the emergency room vets gave her the final injection. Her dark brown eyes glazed over and she slumped into me. I could feel her light body relax. "Good-bye, Spice,"

I told her between sobs. She gave me a last knowing look before the light dimmed from her eyes. And then Larry and I went home to deal with our grief.

About six weeks later, a friend of mine contacted me about some puppies he had from an accidental litter. These pups were distantly related to Spice and he sent me a photo of a white female. I stared at the picture and could hardly believe what I saw: a white puppy with a Greyhound build, tipped ears, and stare-right-through-you-brown eyes. Could this simply be a coincidence? I saw a very old soul stare out at me through those puppy eyes. There was Spice as a puppy. I called up my friend.

"I must have the white female," I told him.

Three weeks later, my friend came to visit us and brought two of the puppies—a male and that female. I held the female and she met my gaze. "I know you," she seemed to say. "We have met before."

I named her Cheyenne, but the eyes I saw were those of Spice. Like Spice, Cheyenne is a spunky lead dog with white fur. When I hold her, Cheyenne gives me that same knowing look that Spice did. Even Larry commented on the similarity between the two dogs. "It's like Spice came back."

My vet was right; it was time to let go. And now Spice has come back to me.

10

Believe in Yourself

I couldn't see ten feet beyond my sled team. It was getting colder and the wind was picking up. It was also growing dark; the sun had passed beyond the cursed mountain I was on. Thick, white flakes pelted my face and lined my hood like a ruff. There was no distinguishing earth and sky; they had blended into a white haze. I was in a whiteout.

Houston, my lead dog, looked back at me, his Beagle-like face in a grimace. Not the most likely sled dog, he was a black and tan throwback to a Gordon Setter ancestor. His parents, I'm told, looked like Huskies. He looked goofy with his flop ears and odd coloring, but was a dynamite lead dog, capable of leading large teams without a fuss. He was in charge of the six-dog team I was running in this race in the middle of a blinding snowstorm.

"What's up, Huey, old boy?" I asked, trying to sound cheerful. Houston gave me his best Eeyore impression, letting his flop ears droop even lower and his tail tuck beneath his legs. His brown eyes met mine and said succinctly, "You're lost, aren't you?"

Actually, I wasn't. Despite the missing trail markers (those damn pie plates they paint with orange Krylon) and despite the childish drawing of the trail the racers had been given (it might have been better if they drew an inverted V with a circle around it to indicate a trail), I knew where I was. I was on the trail that would lead us back to the lodge where I could get hot chocolate and some dinner and the dogs could eat a hot dinner and curl up in a nice, toasty bed. But we weren't going anywhere because Houston decided I had lost my mind.

He has a point, I reflected as I looked up at the sky. The gray was deepening ever so slightly, but there was no way I could see where the trail actually was beyond the ten feet in front of my team. I had to rely solely on my lead dogs, Houston and Cheyenne, to keep us on track. The conditions were treacherous now. We were on a ridge and if the lead dogs made a mistake, we could literally fall off the mountain.

I took a deep breath. The team wasn't cold or tired; they were just dispirited. They'd never been in a whiteout with me before. Hell, I had never been in a whiteout like this. I didn't really blame them for their attitude, but they had no idea that dinner, bed, and everything they desired lay closer ahead than they thought. We had gone maybe eighteen miles out of the twenty-five. It made sense to continue through to the end.

Morale time. I pulled the two snowhooks from the sled and pounded them into the trail. I always use two to anchor my team in case my dogs pull so hard that they pop one out. "Hey there, Huey!" I said as I walked from the sled runners to the lead dogs. Cheyenne, my little white lead, bounced excitedly as I approached. "Stay tight!" I warned her. She almost turned the team, but held on, her brown eyes looking into mine in sheer adoration. "Hey, you guys!" I said. "Don't you want to go home?"

"Go home" is a command mushers sometimes use to convince their team to pick up the speed because they're almost at the finish line. Houston wagged his tail skeptically, but Cheyenne positively melted. *We're almost there?*

"Almost," I crooned. "Let's go home!"

After petting them, I walked down the line. I petted Rigel with his inscrutable blue-eyed gaze, and Calvin, his buddy, who was the loud-mouth of the group. Rigel was a bruiser; as I passed him, he tried to lift his leg on me.

"Rigel!" I growled. He gave me the dog equivalent of a shrug.

Last in line were Miki and Panda in the wheel position, right in front of the sled. They were two dogs I had rescued from the shelter. They were among the seventeen sled dogs confiscated from a fellow who was trying to run a sled dog touring business. They were shy with most people, but loved me. Miki hopped excitedly as I petted them both. They were wolf-gray Huskies. Miki looked like a coyote with his long legs.

After this love fest, I waited. Precious race minutes were ticking away but I had to make sure the dogs were ready. If they weren't, they'd choke and I'd be back where I started. "Ready?" I asked. Miki and Panda hit their harness. Rigel was still eyeing me. Calvin was yapping at Houston, who was turning to look at the crazy woman. Cheyenne was trying to pull but her little body was no match for Houston's size.

"Ready?" I asked.

Three dogs were eager; one dog wasn't paying attention; two dogs thought I had lost my mind.

"Ready?"

Calvin looked at me and realized I was saying something. Then he was barking to go. Houston looked apathetic; Rigel thought I was insane.

"You want to lead, Calvin?" I asked. I walked to Houston and unsnapped his neckline and harness from the tugline and moved him back to Calvin's position. Calvin has led, but he isn't trustworthy. Still, maybe he would lead with Cheyenne. I put him in lead and Houston in Calvin's spot.

I returned to the runners to see, with dismay, that Calvin had turned around and was barking at Houston. "Ready?" I shouted.

Calvin ignored me and kept barking at Houston. Rigel looked at me again like I had lost my mind.

He's right, a little voice inside me said. *I have Mutiny on the Puppy.*

If this were a Jack London story, at this point the musher would beat the hell out of the dogs. But this isn't a Jack London story (I would *never* hit my dogs!), nor can you coerce a sled team to run for you out of fear. The way you train a sled team is through miles of training. We had more than 700 miles of training in just this season, and I hadn't had a real problem.

Until now.

I jumped off the runners and switched Calvin and Rigel. Four lead dogs and not one will lead except Cheyenne. But Cheyenne is young and lacks confidence and won't take the lead by herself.

"Ready?" I almost pleaded when I returned to the runners.

Rigel pounded the harness, much to my relief.

I said a quick prayer to the sled gods, pulled my snowhooks, and hung on. "Hike!" I commanded them.

Rigel and Cheyenne pulled about fifty yards and then stopped. We were at the base of a hill.

I swore. *Could this be any worse?* I wondered. I got off the runners and the team started forward up the hill. I began running alongside through the deep drifts, punching my way through. After awhile I realized I couldn't keep up without riding on the runners of the sled. So I hopped on and the runners sank in the new snow.

The team stopped.

Damn!

"Hike it, Rigel! Hike it, Cheyenne!" I said and started pushing off with my feet (it's called pedaling). We climbed the hill slowly from the ridge through the bowl and up a treeless ridge. Where in the hell were the trail markers?

Suddenly we gained speed. Rigel was pulling like a maniac. "Good Rigel! Good Rigel!" I yelled. And then we came to an abrupt stop and Rigel swung to the left, dragging Cheyenne with him. I saw it and groaned. A small evergreen had dared to peek its way through the drifts. Rigel lifted his leg.

That's when I lost it. "Gawddammit dog!" I shouted. I couldn't change leads on this incline, but I could make him go forward. I stomped up to him, grasped his collar, and started tugging him away from his precious tree. Rigel looked insulted, but I was livid. I took the lead spot, pulling Rigel forward up the hill.

Once we got to the top, we were back in the trees again. I wiped the snow from my eyes with a mittened hand. It was really getting dark. In the gloom, I spied a glint of orange. Rigel was eyeing every tree in the forest. I'm sure he thought he had enough piss to mark each one. I tossed snowhooks down, but I really didn't need them. The whiteout had sunk the dogs' morale to a new low.

I switched Rigel and Houston. I even didn't bother going back to the sled. Instead, I walked with them on the packed trail, through the freshly laid-down powder. I was tired. It was getting dark. I glanced at Houston every so often; he was plodding along. Cheyenne kept looking up.

Then we heard it: a snowmobile. A snowmobile with its lights on came toward my team. I stopped and my team automatically stopped, too. They've heard that sound before and know it's usually someone out looking for us. (This has become a rather common experience.) A man drove up on a red Honda snowmobile and peered at me in the dusk.

"You Maggie Bonham?" he shouted above the engine's whine.

"Yeah," I said. "How much farther is it?"

He looked at me and my dispirited team as if to appraise our ability. "Two miles. But if you turn around, you can get to the road in a half-mile and I can have your husband pick up you and the team."

I looked at my team. Calvin was barking at Houston again. Rigel was eyeing the closest tree. Houston was standing beside me and wagging his tail. He knows a snowmobile means quitting time.

I could be back at the lodge, warm and comfortable. They could be fed and happy, not bored and disheartened. I could be eating a prime rib. They could be nestled in their boxes. All we would have to do is turn back. . . .

Turning back, though, means quitting. If you don't think a dog knows what quitting is, you're sadly mistaken. Like people, sled dogs do understand the difference between quitting and finishing. When they finish, they're often exuberant. When they quit, they do so because morale is low. When a sled dog learns he can end a run that has got him discouraged, he associates tough things with being discouraged and giving up.

I looked the team over with an honest eye. No one was limping. No one was exhausted. No one was injured. Everyone was fine.

"No," I said.

The man on the snowmobile hesitated. "It's only half a mile to the road."

"It's only two miles to the finish line." I fished the headlamp out of my pack and put it on my head. I hit the bumper switch on the battery pack and it lit up. "We're going to finish, dammit. Tell my husband I'm finishing."

"Okay." He shrugged and left.

I was now sure the dogs thought I had lost my mind. They tried to follow the snowmobile, but I held the lead dogs and began walking. One foot in front of the other.

I'd like to say that it was some clever training or a trick I used to get the team going. It wasn't. It was just walking—me walking beside my two lead dogs as the snow came down around us. We walked for a mile and a half.

Then, in the gloom, I saw the parking lot up ahead. I patted each of the dogs and returned to the sled runners. "Houston! Cheyenne! Hike!"

Houston started tentatively, but Cheyenne was pulling for all she could. The feet crawled by. "Good dogs! Go home! Go home!"

Something within my voice suggested urgency. Houston picked up the pace and then we charged out of the forest, into the parking lot, and past the finish line.

The parking lot was mostly empty except for a few trucks. A handful of people were cheering as Houston and Cheyenne broke into a lope and headed for my truck. My husband, Larry, was waiting in full winter gear, as were a handful of people.

"Are the dogs okay?" he asked as he caught Houston and Cheyenne's neckline and hooked them to the truck.

"Yeah—it was a bad whiteout," I said. "They just quit."

One man came up to me, and I presumed he was the race veterinarian. "You want to check my dogs?"

The man shook his head. "I want to check you."

"Huh?"

"For frostbite. I'm a doctor."

"Yeah, sure," I said absently as I began removing Cheyenne's harness. The doctor looked at my face and fingers and proclaimed that I had exceptional cold weather gear.

Not only that, I added silently. *I stayed warm because I had to work.*

We returned to the lodge and I fed the dogs there. The banquet held after this charity race had already started, but I didn't care. The dogs came first. I started ladling out dog kibble mixed with a protein-fat powder and water. The dogs slurped it up, relieved themselves, and waited to go back into their heated boxes in the truck.

Everyone looked good as they snuggled into their straw-filled boxes for a nap while we ate. I threw on some jeans and a sweatshirt and trundled to the banquet.

Once inside, I stared. The banquet hall was huge and dimly lit. Everyone who is anyone from the state was there. People were wearing nice evening dresses, suits, mink coats, and fine jewelry. I stared. I smelled like dogs. I had straw clinging to my jeans. My face was windburned and my jeans and sweatshirt were hardly fashionable. Nor was the hat I had tucked my very windblown hair into.

Did I mention that I smelled like dogs?

Between the dogs and the mountain, I was exhausted, and I walked through the room as if in a dream. Someone found a seat for us in the back. As Larry went to find a waiter to bring us some food, I sat dazed and listened to a distant voice thanking everyone for making this charity race a success.

One woman at the table looked at me. "You're the musher who came in last," she said.

I gulped down some water. (I was dehydrated; I forgot to drink while I was on the trail.) "Yeah."

"Do you even train your dogs?"

I wanted to scream, "Of course, I train my dogs!" I wanted to tell her that she had no clue what mushing was about. That an hour ago I was walking in a blinding snowstorm trying to boost my team's morale. That I was following little pie plates sprayed with Krylon and couldn't tell the difference between the trail and the sky. That my dogs were discouraged because they couldn't see, either, and felt the pressure to perform.

I just looked at her.

She wouldn't understand, even if I tried to explain it to her. How could she? Here within the warm banquet hall in an evening dress and makeup, she had no clue what I had experienced. Unless she got out on the trail, she never would. Thankfully, just then the waiter brought dinner.

As I ate, I looked around at the tables of people and my thoughts wandered back to the trail. Out there, it's real. The cold is real. The danger is real. The trust is real. Something is forged between human and dog out there that can't be expressed in words. Loyalty, trust, and something else far more indescribable.

When Houston nearly gave up, it threatened that bond we have between us. The bond between me and my sled dogs is built on trust. He wasn't willing to trust me that I would safely lead him through, nor did he trust himself that he could finish the race. I knew he wasn't hurt or tired and I knew I had to show him what he really could do.

I don't remember who won the race, nor does it really matter. When I walked out to say goodnight to the dogs before I went to bed, I rubbed each of them behind the ear before putting them back in their boxes. Houston gave me a grin and a tail thump. *We did it.*

I patted him gently. "I know." I smiled as I helped him snuggle into the warm straw. "I know."

Appendix

Treats to Show Your Love

What better way to show your dog you love him than with homemade treats? Dogs love homemade dog biscuits and treats. They know instinctively that you've made the treats just for them, too. (I guess they figure that anything as stinky as liver couldn't be eaten by people!)

Anne Page, the owner of *Houston's Canine Chronicles* newspaper, gave me permission to reprint some of the treats her readers have sent her over the years. While *Canine Chronicles* is no longer published, she was kind enough to give me the recipes anyway.

Apple Cinnamon Training Bits

4 cups whole wheat flour

½ cup cornmeal

2 tablespoons vegetable oil

1 teaspoon cinnamon

1 small apple, grated

1 ⅓ cups water

In a bowl, combine all the ingredients except the apple and water. Add the water to the grated apple in a separate bowl, then add the apple-water mixture to the dry ingredients. Mix until the dough starts coming together. Turn out onto a lightly floured surface. Knead well. Roll out into a rectangle about ¼ inch to ½ inch thick. Take a straight edge and score the dough horizontally and vertically to make a grid of ¾-inch squares. Be careful to score only the surface of the dough—do not completely cut through.

Place the scored dough on a baking sheet that has been sprayed with a nonstick spray. Bake in a preheated 325°F oven for 1 hour. Cool on a wire rack. When cool, break off pieces along the scored lines.

Canine Cookie Bones

2 cups water

1 pound beef liver

1 ½ cups toasted wheat germ

1 ½ cups whole wheat flour

In a 2-quart pan, bring the water to a boil over high heat and add the liver. Reduce the heat, cover, and simmer until the liver is no longer pink in the center (about 10 minutes). Pour through a strainer held over a bowl, reserving 1 cup of the liquid. Cut the liver into 1-inch pieces.

Put the liver in a blender or food processor. Add the reserved liquid and whirl until the mixture is smoothly puréed. Scrape into a bowl. Stir in the wheat germ and flour until they are well moistened. Turn onto a lightly floured board and roll out the dough to ½-inch thickness for large bones. Cut the dough with a bone-shaped cookie cutter.

Place the bones 1 ½ inches apart on a lightly greased baking sheet. Bake in a preheated 350°F oven until browned, about 20 minutes. Turn off the heat and let the bones cool in the oven at least three hours. Refrigerate in an airtight container up to two weeks; freeze for longer storage.

Carob Treats

3 cups whole wheat flour

2 ½ cups uncooked oatmeal

2 ounces carob chips, melted

½ cup powdered milk

½ cup wheat germ

1 tablespoon brown sugar

1 cup water

½ cup molasses

⅛ cup corn oil or margarine

⅛ cup peanut oil

Mix the flour, oatmeal, carob chips, powdered milk, wheat germ, and brown sugar in a large bowl. Add the remaining ingredients and mix until the dough is blended (it will be stiff). Cover the dough with plastic wrap and chill. Roll the dough out ½ inch thick on a lightly floured board. Cut into shapes.

Transfer to a lightly greased cookie sheet and bake in a preheated 300°F oven for 1 hour. Cool on a wire rack.

Cheese Nuggets

1 cup uncooked oatmeal

¼ cup margarine

1 ½ cups hot water or meat juices

½ cup powdered milk

1 cup grated cheddar cheese

¼ teaspoon salt

1 egg, beaten

1 cup wheat germ

1 cup cornmeal

3 cups whole wheat flour

Combine the oatmeal and margarine in a large bowl and pour hot water over them; let stand 5 minutes. Stir in the milk, cheese, salt, and egg. Then add the wheat germ and cornmeal and mix well. Add the flour ½ cup at a time. Knead three to four minutes. Add more flour until the dough is stiff. Roll the dough out ½ inch thick on a lightly floured board. Cut into shapes.

Transfer to a lightly greased cookie sheet and bake in a preheated 300°F oven for 1 hour. Turn off the heat and let the bones cool in the oven 1½ hours.

Cheese and Garlic Cookies

1 ¼ cups grated cheddar cheese

¼ pound corn oil margarine, softened

1 clove garlic, crushed

pinch of salt

1 ½ cups whole wheat flour

milk

Grate the cheese and let it stand until it reaches room temperature. In a large bowl, cream the cheese with the softened margarine, garlic, salt, and flour. Add enough milk to form the dough into a ball. Cover with plastic wrap and chill for half an hour. Roll the dough out ½ inch thick on a lightly floured board. Cut into shapes.

Transfer to a lightly greased cookie sheet and bake in a preheated 375°F oven for 15 minutes or until lightly browned and firm. Cool on a wire rack.

Sunflower Dog Biscuits

2 cups whole wheat flour

½ cup soy flour

1 teaspoon salt

¼ cup cornmeal

¼ cup sunflower seeds

2 tablespoons butter or vegetable oil

¼ cup molasses

2 eggs mixed with ¼ cup milk, plus more milk

In a large bowl, mix the flours, salt, cornmeal, and sunflower seeds. Add the melted butter or oil, molasses, and egg mixture. (Reserve 1 tablespoon of the egg mixture.) Knead together. If the dough is too stiff, add more milk. Cover with plastic wrap and chill for half an hour. Roll the dough out ½ inch thick on a lightly floured board. Cut into desired shapes with a cookie cutter.

Transfer to a lightly greased cookie sheet and brush the tops with the remaining egg mixture. Bake in a preheated 350°F oven for 30 minutes. Cool on a wire rack. Store in a tightly sealed container.

Savory Dog Biscuits

1 cup whole wheat flour mixed with 1 cup all-purpose flour

½ cup powdered milk

6 tablespoons margarine or shortening

½ cup wheat germ

1 teaspoon brown sugar

1 egg

½ teaspoon salt

½ cup water

1 teaspoon garlic powder

1 teaspoon grated carrot

1 teaspoon grated cheese

In a large bowl, combine flours, milk, margarine, and wheat germ and mix until it resembles cornmeal. Beat the brown sugar into the egg. Add salt and water to the egg mixture. Gradually stir the egg mixture into the flour to form a stiff dough. Add the remaining ingredients and knead. Roll the dough out ½ inch thick on a lightly floured board. Cut into desired shapes with a cookie cutter.

Transfer to a lightly greased cookie sheet. Bake in a preheated 325°F oven for 30 minutes. Cool on a wire rack. Store in a tightly sealed container.

Sharon's Liver Cake Cookies

1 pound cooked chicken livers, mashed

½ cup cornmeal

2 tablespoons garlic, crushed

1 cup whole wheat flour

In a large bowl, mix together all ingredients. The dough will be soft and sticky. Spread the dough on a lightly greased cookie sheet. Bake in a preheated 350°F oven until dry. Cool on a wire rack and break into pieces.

Microwave Dog Biscuits

½ cup all-purpose flour

¾ cup powdered milk

½ cup quick-cooking rolled oats

¼ cup yellow cornmeal

1 teaspoon sugar

⅓ cup shortening

1 egg, lightly beaten

1 tablespoon instant bouillon granules

½ cup hot water

In a medium bowl, combine the flour, powdered milk, oats, corn-meal, and sugar. Cut in the shortening until the mixture resembles coarse crumbs. Add the egg and stir.

Mix the bouillon with the hot water and stir until it dissolves. Slowly pour the bouillon into the flour mixture and beat with a fork until all is moistened. Form the dough into a ball and knead on a floured board for 5 minutes or until smooth and elastic.

Divide the dough in half and roll out each half to about ½ inch thick. Cut out shapes with cookie cutters. Alternatively, you can roll the dough into two 1-inch-diameter logs and cut off ½-inch pieces.

Arrange 6 cut-out shapes or 24 nuggets on a 10-inch microwave-safe plate. Microwave at 50 percent (medium) for 5 to 10 minutes or until the biscuits are firm and dry to the touch. Rotate the plate every two minutes and turn shapes over halfway through the cooking time.

About the Author

Maggie Bonham is a writer and sled dog racer who lives in Colorado. She has been a professional writer since 1995 and has sixteen current and upcoming books to her credit. Her articles have appeared in several national publications, including *Dog Fancy, Your Dog, Catnip, DogWorld, Dog & Kennel, Pet Life, PetView, Natural Pet, OnSiteFitness*, and *Mushing Magazine*. She has been a columnist and contributing editor for *Dog & Kennel* and *PetView* magazines and was a frequent contributor to Pets.com, TheDog Daily.com, and Vetmedcenter.com Web sites. She is also the author of *Prophecy of Swords*, a fantasy novel.

Maggie is a three-time winner of the prestigious Maxwell Award from the Dog Writers Association of America for writing excellence, and the winner of the Pet-Sitters International First-Canine Award for the most humorous story told from a dog's perspective. She trains various breeds and competes in agility, sled dog racing, obedience, and conformation. She currently lives with seventeen dogs of various breeds and mixes, and one cat. Visit her Web site at www.shadowhelm.net.

Photo Credits

Photo pp. 2, 3, 4, 5, 8, 11, 65, 122, 138, 172, 182, Bonham; pp. 14, 23, 67, 69, 72, 129, Faust; p. 16, Bigos; pp. 32, 99, 103, 111, 134, Risdon; p. 35, Robertson; pp. 37, 40, 47, 79, 132, Bullard; p. 45, 80, 86, 116, 152, Peters-Mayer; pp. 84, 109, 144, Richtsmeier; p. 76, Meleski; p. 91, Przywara; p. 126, Holowinski/Bonham; p. 128, Taylor; p. 141, Drossman; pp. 146, 150, 178, Stabler; p. 155, DeGioia